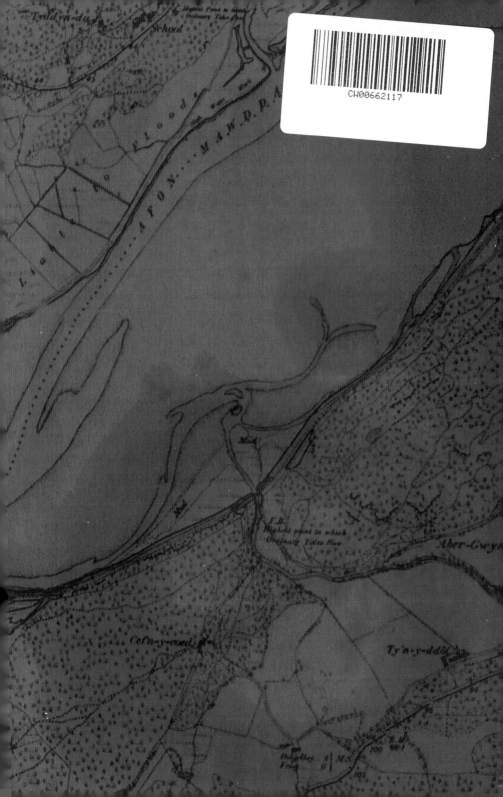

Dedicated to
the QM staff
who have
driven, cooked,
washed and wiped,
yomped and cajoled
on Farchynys duties
since 1963

First published 2017

Strategol Publishing
Imprint of Strategic Leaps
Southridge, 5 Butts Road, Horspath
Oxford, OX33 1RH

www.artfulstrategy.com

Printed in the UK.

Marians on the Mawddach

An English school's love affair with a Welsh estuary

Compiled and edited by
PAUL CHRISTOPHER WALTON

"Traditions and stories,
the salt of life,
are passing away,
because there is
no one to tell them
in a way that busy
pre-occupied people
have time or inclination
to listen to."

TP Ellis Dolgelley and Llanelltyd, 1928

1. Floreat Reginae

The opening line of the school song is "Floreat Reginae Schola Mariae" – May Queen Mary's School flourish.

Foreword

For generations of Marians, Farchynys, our Welsh Centre on the Mawddach, has been a pair of lungs. Spending a weekend in Wales allows pupils and staff to breathe deeply the sea and mountain air and return to Walsall feeling inspired and invigorated. The Coach House has done more than we might realise to keep Queen Mary's School healthy, not only in body, but also in mind and spirit.

The school's success rests on four pillars. We say that we are *academic in purpose*. Farchynys reminds us that the great outdoors is a great classroom. Intellectual curiosity takes hold in exciting ways on the Estuary beach, on the Coed-y-Brenin forest trails, on the battlements of Harlech Castle.

We aim to be *international in outlook*. Having a foothold in Wales reminds us that different languages and cultures – a different nation – can be found on our doorstep. Coming down the other side of Dinas, we see road signs that tell us to "arafach nawr." It's good advice: slowing down allows us to see things differently.

Our third pillar prompts us to be *enterprising in spirit*. The Coach House provides the space and opportunity to develop fresh ideas, prompting pupils to shape an initiative, assume responsibility, take the lead. Enterprise can take various forms: it might look like a Fustie-designed, home-baked pizza one week and a CCF improvised bivouac on the Headland the next.

Finally, we count ourselves privileged to lay claim to being *generous in approach*. Farchynys stands as a monument to Marian generosity. Gifts of money got the project off the ground and have allowed us to maintain the Centre for more than half a century, but it's not all about hard cash: every corner of the estate is a reminder of the imaginative invention and sheer hard work of so many members of the QM community.

I am hugely grateful to Paul Walton for this book; he embodies the spirit of the place. Thanks to him, and many like him, I am confident that there will be Marians on the Mawddach for generations to come. My hope is that Farchynys will continue to inspire them, giving them a bracing blast of the air of life – life to the full.

Timothy Swain, Headmaster, March 2017

1963 and all that

T This is the story of a place, a singularly beautiful place; and a school, an old, illustrious school that discovered exciting new classrooms to nurture its pupils in this ancient landscape.

The place is the Mawddach, a magnificent river surrounded by mountains built on the debris of mountains that flows into the sea at Abermaw, the town known to the English as Barmouth. Located in the historic county of Merioneth, now Gwynedd, the writer Jessica Lofthouse called the Estuary, "the best ten miles in Britain."

The Mawddach Estuary

The school is Queen Mary's Grammar School, found one hundred miles away in Walsall, in what is now the West Midlands, but which, at the time of its foundation in July 1554 by Queen Mary Tudor, was a significant town in the county of Staffordshire.

The comparison between a mountainous and sparsely populated estuary which hard-core geomorphologists are more likely to identify as a 'drowned embayment located on the southern flank of the Harlech dome', and the concrete industrial heartland of England could not be more dramatic. But in this contrast magic happened – and still happens today, flowing naturally from the powerful interaction between people and place. After all, estuaries are transitional zones and the inflows of both salt and fresh water provide high levels of nutrients, making them amongst the most productive natural habitats in the world. The

Mawddach has helped grow generations of Queen Mary's folk and this book tells some of their stories.

But the history of Marians – as we call the past and present pupils of Queen Mary's – on the Mawddach does not begin with the arrival of the first convoy from Walsall in 1963, but rather a hundred years earlier, when, to great rejoicing and the sound of a brass band, the magnificent railway viaduct at Barmouth was finally opened, bringing with it the first mass invasion of the English on to the streets of Y Bermo.

There were two competing railway lines heading for the Mawddach: The Aberystwyth and Welsh Coast railway from Aberystwyth and Machynlleth, and the Great Western from Bala and Ruabon. Before they arrived, this part of Wales had been impenetrable and dangerous. Beyond the border, boggy moorlands and unwelcoming mountains

The Royal Arms and Personal Badge of Mary I

provided an effective natural barrier. Roads were poor and posed risks to travellers – during the 16th century, Dinas Mawddwy had been terrorised by the infamous Red Bandits.

By the beginning of the nineteenth century, the area was beginning to become interesting, especially to well-heeled travellers and their artist chums looking for adventure after European grand tours had been halted by war and plague. The discovery of gold at Clogau in the 1840s created yet more buzz to the booming slate mining business. But it was the arrival of the railways in the 1860s that changed the local economy forever.

Leading the charge of the Victorians who discovered the area's charms were the industrial barons from Birmingham and Manchester, who arrived intent on spending their booty purchasing suitable country estates in Snowdonia. Fairbourne owes its existence to the magnate behind McDougall's self-raising flour. Lea and Perrins Worcestershire Sauce built St. John's the Evangelist in Barmouth. And the founder of Bird's Custard built himself a villa at Criccieth - painted in an appropriate shade of buttery yellow, of course.

Another of these industrialists was to play a vital role in our story. In 1870, a Cheshire cotton mill owner, convalescing in the area, purchased some land for a summer residence that he wanted to build near Bontddu, a small hamlet between Dolgellau and Barmouth. The mill owner was called Thomas Oliver and the estate he bought on the Mawddach Estuary in

Barmouth Bridge, loco with steam wreath

the gap between two mountains – Y Vigra and Cadair Idris – was called Farchynys.

The story now shifts in place and time to post-war Walsall in the 1950s, when the free grammar school of Queen Mary was having a splendid renaissance after celebrating its quatercentenary in 1954. The arrival of a new Headmaster, S L Darby, in 1956 proved to be another decisive moment in the history of the school. Sam Darby combined a steely intellectual core – he had been a Classics scholar at New College – with a terrific sense of ambition and a gift for politics and diplomacy. Intent on driving change at Queen Mary's, he spent the rest of his career expanding the horizons of those within the school and successfully defending it against challengers from without.

In 1962, Sam returned to Oxford for a conference where one of the talks was to be given by the renowned Kurt Hahn. Born in Berlin to Jewish parents, he had spoken out against Nazi Stormtroopers and had had to exit Germany fast as a consequence. He arrived in Great Britain with an educational philosophy that mixed Platonic logic with Cistercian austerity, as well as a belief in the value of physical fitness and outdoor adventure. He founded Gordonstoun School, where Prince Philip, the Duke of Edinburgh, was educated and inspired, and also set up the Outward Bound Organisation. In the year that Sam met him in Oxford, Hahn, 56, had just founded Atlantic College, one of the first places to offer the International Baccalaureate.

Sam, himself a keen student of Plato, found Hahn's ideas compelling and wrote in one of his first Welsh Centre welcome speeches:

"Hahn propounded the theme that education involved the whole man, and the challenges of sea, of mountain, of social service as well as intellect were important constituents which we neglect at our peril in bringing up the young."

For Sam, the seed had been planted. Before long, that seed would grow strong at Farchynys.

Looking back from the present day, what was extraordinary about the scale of Sam Darby's ambition and vision in 1962 was that, at exactly the same time that Hahn was lighting the blue touch paper of Darby's Project Outward-Bound, the Headmaster's mind was already fully occupied with the plans to move the school from its Victorian brownstone quarters in Walsall town centre to the green fields of Mayfield on the leafy outskirts – a massive undertaking. But somehow, Sam found the energy and the time to embark on a charm offensive in search of money. In a matter of weeks he had found a number of old boys prepared to help finance the Outward Bound project. The original donors included Messrs J Aspinall, Norman and Ted Franks, R Wiggin, Douglas Gilbert, L E Podmore, A Stephens, Frank Stretton, Harold Taylor, R B White, Henry

Kurt Hahn and Sam Darby

Wilkins and Frank Wootton. Each of these gents was persuaded to provide £200 for an unlimited period.

A search for a suitable location and property was soon under way. Scouting parties identified a variety of places within Snowdonia National Park, still a relatively new institution having been founded in 1951. One building quickly stood out as favourite: a dilapidated building known as The Coach House, just off the Dolgellau to Barmouth road on the Farchynys estate that Thomas Oliver had built long ago as a summer home. Sam and his team thought it had great potential, but saw it would need a considerable amount of work to make it fit for purpose.

Sam got to work on the great and the good of Walsall and had quickly mobilised a number of them to be members of his Welsh Centre Management Committee. Prominent local solicitor and Old Marian Philip Evans was persuaded to be Minute Secretary, and all historians of Queen Mary's should be for ever grateful to Phil for the comprehensiveness of his notes and the quality of his handwriting. Phil always referred to the new QMGS Welsh Centre as Farch Ynys – two separate words that in Welsh mean "Isle of horses." Today Farchynys isn't an island of course, but the name does reflect the tendency of the area to inundation and flooding.

With the help of his committee and the usual Darby charm, Sam soon had promises of interest-free loans, which allowed the school to purchase The Coach House for £1,675 and 10 acres of land for £300. The parcel included part of the Headland, with superb views over the Estuary. But now Sam needed to make it habitable.

Without the help of the Old Boys (Queen Mary's Club) and the parents (Queen Mary's Association), The Welsh Centre would never have happened. Parents with the requisite skills readily volunteered their services. Bob Christie, a local architect, drew up some plans

Plaque celebrating Kurt Hahn

and Harold Taylor, a Bloxwich builder, undertook all the significant reconstruction work. Kitchens and lavatories were ripped out, a new kitchen and shower room installed, new windows were fitted and a back staircase created.

As well as the refurbishment of the property shell, the Welsh Centre Committee worked tirelessly throughout 1962 exploring a whole range of other operational issues: transport and insurance; utilities including water supply and telephone; and the fixtures, fittings and equipment necessary to support fieldwork and adventure training. The original plan assumed the termly programme would consist of four weeks for the CCF, two for the Scouts, two for the Duke of Edinburgh's Award and three for subject field courses such as Geography. The Walsall After War Committee was approached for surplus kit, and the CCF Top Brass asked to check their stores.

The opening of The Coach House, 1963

The prominente of Walsall were invited to check their garages and attics for anything useful. Mrs Bull gave a sideboard; Mrs Nash, an easy chair. Mr Grove gave a canoe; Mr Plater, an outboard motor. The wonderful ladies of the QMA (always celebrated with superlatives) provided pillows, and the CCF Brass did provide some bunk beds, even though Phil Evans was to note later that they were "less than successful." Of course, cash was just as acceptable, if not more so, should friends have no surplus kit to hand.

Thus did it come to pass that on the 23rd November 1963, the first QMGS expeditionary force left Walsall for Merioneth, carrying with it all of the impedimenta that Sam Darby and Phil Bull, the newly appointed first Warden of Farchynys, had been able to blag. On arriving at The Coach House, the party had a somewhat comedic moment when the key to the front door could not be immediately identified from the collection it had just acquired.

But all teething troubles had been sorted when, six months later, Sam Darby, flanked by his donors, his committee, his parent volunteers and *The Walsall Observer* presided over the official opening of The Coach House, by which time 163 boys and 12 masters had already paid their first visits to the Estuary.

The second great English invasion of the Mawddach was now under way.

Abermaw

Summer, 2013

Tonight I walked along the estuary of my youth,
Saw water colour landscapes of hope and fear
Watched the family outline in the surf,
Smelt the kelp and tasted salt once more;
Heard the white noise of waves breaking at the bar,
The tinkle of dinghy bells,
The relentless nagging of the gulls,
The flap of ice cream banners in deserted cabins,
And witnessed the sun's last defiant blaze,
As a crescent moon rose above Tyrau Mawr.

Autumn, 1968

A misty evening in November,
Waiting for the minibus
At the old signal box in Bermo;
A pocketful of birthday money
Eating the posh nougat
(We pronounced it the Anglo-Saxon way of course),
Shivering, happy and ambitious.

2. This is what they teach us – memories of QM masters and staff

The Farchynys experience would not have been possible without the whole-hearted contribution of time, energy and expertise from the staff of Queen Mary's. From the earliest visits, the traditions initiated by Messrs Bull, Archer, Dickson et al have been passed on to generations of staff members. And the effect of Farchynys has not been purely one way. The power of the place on people is palpable in these short extracts contributed by former QM Masters.

Discovering a
new dimension

A few thoughts on Farchynys

My first acquaintance with The Coach House was in early 1979, shortly after my appointment to the Headship of Queen Mary's. My visit, with the then Headmaster, Sam Darby, opened up a whole new dimension to the life of the school. Sam was an enthusiastic guide, pointing out both the majesty of Cadair Idris and the beauty of the Mawddach Estuary.

One of my early visits to The Coach House was for a choral concert to Barmouth - the whole choir, under the baton of Beverley Wragg, in a performance of Handel's *Messiah*. Accompanied by Geoff Weaver, a former colleague of mine and organist and master of the choristers at Bradford Cathedral, the performance was not just a great success: it helped to cement relations between the school and local people.

I would go back many times, including for the annual visit by the Parents' Association (The QMA) – always of particular interest for the parents of first-year boys ("Fusties"). These visits helped encourage pupils and parents to make good use of Farchynys, to the great benefit of so many.

In the early 1980s, I remember weekend visits with pupils, parents and governors to clear rhododendron from the hill behind The Coach House. One old Marian, Hugh Homer, even bought a winch to help! **[Editor's note: for more on this please see the War of the Rhodies on page 93]**

It is difficult to overestimate the importance of the part played (and still played) by so many pupils, staff and parents. A lifelong debt is due to all who have played an active part in the development and experience of Farchynys.

Keith Howard, Headmaster 1978–1995

An (almost) A–Z guide to Farchynys

A
ARUP?
Are you up?

B
Breath-taking first view of the estuary on approach.

C
Call to meals, heralded by the sound of a large saucepan lid being beaten.

Chores on the duty rota. The favourite 'end of visit' chore was, of course, cleaning the toilets!

D
Dingbats. A legend about vampire bats at Farchynys and told to Fusties by prefects as they set off on a torch-lit night time walk on the Headland. The legend became fact when we found the bat cave and rogue bats in dorm sinks.

Duty rota. Drawn up and posted on the dayroom noticeboard at the start of each visit, the rota showed a list of the various chores to be done and the group(s) (chosen at random) assigned to the job.

F
Fire practice. Held on every visit. If going-to-bed noise carried on in the dorm for too long, we'd hold the practice just as everyone was settling down to sleep, meaning they'd have to assemble outside in pyjamas.

G
Girls at Farchynys. In later years, girls joined the sixth form. They slept in the larger of the two staff bedrooms and shared the staff bathroom.

Glow-worms. An amazing sight when lining the driveway. Rather disappointing when examined in the lab.

H
Halfway House pub. Nothing more needs to be said!

Leftovers. In the early days the wonderful ladies in the QM kitchens would provide us with any leftover food in large aluminium containers – main course, sweet including that perennial favourite – chocolate concrete"). These made welcome contribution to the food budget. Things are done differently these days.

etting your hair down – archynys is a real "getting to now you" place: a chance to e pupils and staff in totally ifferent light.

stening to Mahler (below) fter a late night/early morning nd to a Lab session on Biology eld trips.

Mai the Milk of the Old Smithy, Bontddu. We simply couldn't have managed without her! Not only did she supply us with crate(s) of milk ready for our arrival, she'd top up our supplies if we ran short during a field course. Mai also cleaned The Coach House after each visit, was a fount of knowledge about the area, and knew most of the QM staff very well - they were always welcome at her place for a cosy chat in front of a warm fire.

Maybugs. It was often very hot in the lab on summer field trips and all the windows were open. As it got dark the tremendous clattering and painful impact of these large heavy beetles (cockchafers) was most unwelcome!

Mudflats (see 'Suckering')

Night sky. Total blackness with no pollution from city lights – just made for stargazing.

Orienteering – or not, as the case may be. Common errors included turning the map upside down, or following a route with the river or other landmark on the wrong side of the path!

Porridge. The Yates Porridge Readiness Test: the stirring spoon must stand upright unaided! "One slice or two?"

Quadwants. Ken Yates could not pronounce 'r's so he told the students to mark out half-metre 'quadwants' for plant identification He was affectionately teased about this difficulty and given 'exercises' to say e.g. River Ribble. He greatly enjoyed the ribbing.

R Rhododendron culling – excellent fuel for the staff room fire.

Round-the-table table tennis. All the usual table tennis rules applied, plus the Hit and Run Round Table Rule. Strictly no table tennis bats – but anything else was OK, from books, to saucepan lids.

S Suckering pupils on salt marsh mudflats. During the sessions on the estuary mudflats, Ken would stride off, ostensibly to find the best place to dig for 'inhabitants'. Eventually he would signal to us to follow, only for us to end up wallowing in up to 40cm of soft mud, unable to walk without removing our wellies. Conveniently, Ken would always have his camera at the ready.

T "Thanks for taking us" always nice to hear at the end of a visit.

Tranquillity – the silence and superb relaxation that followed a day's activity.

**Gordon Brudenell,
Staff 1960–1994**

W Water supply. Initially there was no mains water and the viability of any visit depended on a report on the level of water in the hillside tank at the end of the previous visit (with any update from Mai).

Welshpool – the 'obligatory' stop for tuck and 'supplies'.

Y Y is for Yates: Ken Yates **(above).** 'The Laird of Farchynys', easy to spot in his deerstalker hat, stick, ever at-the-ready camera and wellies. Ken was in his element at Farchynys – truly relaxed and extremely happy. Field trips (Biology and Geology), first year weeks, year weekends – whatever he could go on, he was there! I accompanied him on very many of these visits. He was always superb company and pupils of all ages had a great time. He liked to spend Christmas at The Coach House, walking, reading and listening to his extensive classical music collection.

Mai the Milk

Stuart Holtam remembers a wonderful friend

Mrs Clarke, known fondly as 'Mai the Milk' because she did the daily milk round between Barmouth and Dolgellau, was a great friend and supporter of the school. She took over as caretaker and cleaner at Farchynys in the 1970s, and kept an eye on things for us when The Coach House was not in use. But she was much more than a caretaker to many of us, and she was worth her weight in Welsh gold to the school.

She and her husband, Desmond, became personal friends of many members of staff. No Farchynys visit was complete for some of us without dropping into their home, Yr Efail (The Old Smithy) next door to the Halfway House in Bontddu, sitting by the open fire with her black Labrador at our feet, and having a chat over a cup of tea. We caught up on the local gossip – and there was always plenty of that – while she kept up to date with developments at the school and the people she knew at our end. Her soft, gentle Welsh lilt was always a delight to listen to, and a reminder that English was her second language. As our families grew, we took our children to meet her, got to know her son, Brian and, eventually, met her grandchildren.

Mai spent her life in Bontddu and lived in her parents' house, where her father had been the village smith. Her milk round brought her into contact with nearly all the residents of the northern slopes of the Mawddach, and there were few people in the area she didn't know, even if they weren't customers. She was well respected in the local community, and she liked us, so stood up for us; this was especially comforting during a potentially difficult time when there was a resurgence in Welsh nationalism and some English second homes in North Wales were burnt.

In the days before seven-day timers, she would switch on the central heating at The Coach House before every party arrived, and leave 20 pints of milk in the fridge – in glass bottles of course. The last act of every school party until the 1990s was to call in at Mai's as they drove through Bontddu on the return journey to Walsall, drop off the empties in their crate, and pay her for the milk.

When Desmond died, I attended his funeral as both a friend of the family and a representative of the school. The service was held at the little church hidden away at Caerdeon, between Farchynys and Barmouth, and the singing of the Welsh hymns was magnificent and moving. His grave was near the bottom of the steeply sloping churchyard, and during the interment the congregation was arrayed among the gravestones above it, like a scene in a film. Several years later, I was also privileged to attended Mai's funeral; she rests with Desmond, still at home in her valley.

FRIENDS AND NEIGHBOURS

From the arrival of Queen Mary's on the Mawddach in 1963, the Head and Mr Bull, the first Warden, were intent upon creating good links with the community. Local people were contracted to help run and maintain The Coach House. In 1974, when the Field Laboratory extension was conceived, a local builder was engaged to build it and when it was unveiled as the Cadair Idris room, neighbours and dignitaries from Dolgellau, Bontddu and Barmouth were invited as VIPs. CCF exercises depended on the support of local farmers and the Jones family at Fridd-bryn-Côch became particular friends of the school. As Beverley Wragg describes, the Chamber Choir forged close links with local churches in Barmouth and Dolgellau, where several choral concerts were given and much appreciated, and the choir sang Christmas carols for neighbours including Alan and Ruth Fisher at Farchynys Hall. [Editor's note: Mrs Fisher is now a sprightly 88 and gave me an excellent crash course in Welsh pronunciation].

Mai 'the Milk' was a much loved and thoughtful woman who did far more than just deliver milk and who played a vital role in keeping Farchynys fully functional. Not surprising for a school with a specialisation in languages, QM has a strong sensitivity to the Welsh language, and to this day pupils are reminded of it throughout The Coach House, where rooms and equipment are labelled in Welsh.

This is what they teach us

Penmaen Pool

From the Visitors' Book at the Inn

Who long for rest, who look for pleasure
Away from counter, court, or school
O where live well your lease of leisure
But here at, here at Penmaen Pool?

You'll dare the Alp? You'll dart the skiff?
Each sport has here its tackle and tool:
Come, plant the staff by Cadair cliff;
Come; swing the sculls on Penmaen Pool.

What's yonder? Grizzled Dyphwys dim:
The triple-hummocked Giant's stool,
Hoar messmate, hobs and nobs with him
To halve the bowl of Penmaen Pool.

And all the landscape under survey,
At tranquil turns, by nature's rule,
Rides repeated topsy-turvy
In frank, in fairy Penmaen Pool.

And Charles's Wain, the wondrous seven,
And sheep-flock clouds like worlds of wool.
For all they shine so, high in heaven,
Shew brighter shaken in Penmaen Pool.

The Mawddach, how she trips! Though throttled
If floodtide teeming thrills her full,
And mazy sands all water-wattled
Waylay her at ebb, past Penmaen Pool.

But what's to see in stormy weather,
When grey showers gather and gusts are cool?
Why, raindrop-roundels looped together
That lace the face of Penmaen Pool.

Then even in weariest wintry hour
Of New Year's month or surly Yule
Furred snows, charged tuft above tuft, tower
From darksome darksome Penmaen Pool.

And ever, if bound here hardest home,
You've parlour-pastime left and (who'll
Not honour it?) ale like goldy foam
That frocks an oar in Penmaen Pool.

Then come who pine for peace or pleasure
Away from counter, court, or school,
Spend here your measure of time and treasure
And taste the treats of Penmaen Pool.

Gerard Manley-Hopkins

Ken's natural habitat

Steve Law pays tribute to Ken Yates (aka Stiffo)

F rom the moment he arrived at the school in 1967, Ken's second home was The Coach House at Farchynys. Indeed, I suspect he would gladly have made it his principal one. Always dressed in wellies, an orange oilskin jacket and a deerstalker hat, his knowledge of salt marsh vegetation and the birdlife of the Mawddach Estuary was legendary.

My first visit with Ken was on a Biology field course over Easter 1971. I remember, Tony Wiggin had brought his entire family with, so Ken spent the weekend sleeping in the Warden's Office.

"Virtually every time I go to Farchynys I will mention his name, or simply think of him, or call on him to remind me of a plant's name"

The following Whit Holiday, many of us in the Biology set persuaded him to take us out exploring. Walking with him, my knowledge of butterflies and birds improved no end. He'd take us into Barmouth every night to the Cors y Gedol hotel to drink Guinness and play snooker. On field courses he had to, so that Wiggin could get the kids to bed!

I returned with him as the cook boy on Biology field courses after Gordon Brudenell retired. In turn, he became cook boy on my Geology field courses. We were both enthusiastic lay students of each other's subjects: I learned loads about sand dune vegetation and succession, ferns and seaweed zonation; in turn, he picked up on my geological knowledge.

On later courses, when Biology students asked how I knew so much, I'd reply that I'd been on Biology field courses with Ken Yates, and paid attention.

He was a man with a wicked sense of humour. A boy on a Biology Field Course asked me what I liked about Farchynys. "Depends on the season," I answered. "In spring, yellow flowers - primroses, daffs, celandines; in the summer, rhodies and azalias - and the red valerian." I was just about to move into autumn when Ken interrupted: "Oh do shut up, Law!"

Ken Yates 1944–1999 (Staff 1967–1998)

One of his lovable traits was to allow his favourite fruit crumble and thick custard, which he insisted I make, to go cold on top of the fireplace in the staff room. He would return to it some hours later and have it as a late night snack.

His visits in the '80s and '90s involved weekends of Now Get Out Of That problems but really he wanted to indulge in listening to classic music - Mahler and Wagner - with the likes of Bev Wragg and Graham Larkin.

He'd go up to Farchynys over the Christmas holiday, listen to his music and walk the walks. I found his sunset photo on the shortest day of the year from the Headland truly emotional and would always use it to finish my Farchynys Year 7 parents' talk.

He was a dedicated man who introduced me to the real pleasures of Farchynys – as well as the biological bits. He was very private, but I managed to glean a lot of information from him that others couldn't. When Ken retired, he insisted that I have all his slides of sand dune and salt marsh vegetation. They are a treasured possession.

Virtually every time I go to Farchynys I will mention his name, or simply think of him, or call on him to remind me of a plant's name. He was a great influence and a wonderful companion and mentor.

[Editor's note: Ken Yates died in 1999. Those who knew him will remember the joy Farchynys brought him].

Steve Law, QM 1965-1977, Staff 1977-2012, Warden 1995-2012

Sexy Bexy makes a clean sweep!

An early weekend at The Coach House

served as an officer in the Combined Cadet Force, following my earlier National Service with the Royal Corps of Signals. And in an era of emerging household appliances – including, of course, the Bex-Bissell carpet sweeper – what nickname could have been more appropriate for me than 'Bex'? Perhaps they thought that I would take anything in, without always making a clean sweep!

My wife, Jennifer, and I remember our Outward Bound weekends at Farchynys in the 1960s, with a group of perhaps eight eager sixth formers – not always from the CCF – and the Friday preparations that would be needed to get the party underway. Jennifer would have ordered and collected a huge box of groceries from Moseley's, stretching out a very small allowance for the whole group. By 4.30pm the minibus would be ready to leave.

"Perhaps they thought that I would take anything in, without always making a clean sweep!"

The staff quarters at Farchynys, a bedroom and bathroom, were separated from the boys' dormitory by a relatively thin wall that allowed sounds to be transferred either way. Getting ready for bed on the first night, I visited the bathroom and pulled the flush on the toilet. Hardly had the noise of the flush died away then a voice could be heard proclaiming from the dormitory, "We can hear you, Bexy. Sexy Bexy!"

Brian Bissell, QM 1944–1952 and Staff, Head of R.E. with Geography and Current Affairs 1961–1966

Marians on the Mawddach   *23*

A firm
foothold at Farchynys

Stuart Holtam's memories and reflections

O
n my first visit to The Coach House, as a brand new teacher in October 1972, `I was instantly won over to Farchynys and its potential. I also somehow managed to survive climbing Snowdon in smooth-soled, elastic sided, suede Hush Puppies (I had forgotten my boots).

Sam Darby offered me the job of Warden during the Autumn Term of 1978, shortly before he retired. His successor, Keith Howard, gave me a remarkably free rein as Warden; I've no doubt that my growing sense of ownership for our Welsh annexe gave me an appetite for – and many of the skills needed – to become, first Deputy Head, then Head.

* * *

I visited Farchynys more with Steve Law than with any other member of staff. After John Vallance donated the first Farchynys Log Book, Steve would disappear to the staff bathroom for about an hour on the final morning of our visits, to write up a detailed account of proceedings. I was left to organise the reluctant pupils and supervise the clearing up.

* * *

Geography field courses in the company of Brian Edwards were a particular pleasure. Not for him a bright orange cagoule, waterproof over-trousers and walking boots: he would put on his wellies, then his brown overcoat, open his umbrella, and set off up the hill at a startling pace, despite his limp. He was erudite and fluent, but always to the point: a great inspiration to teachers as well as pupils.

* * *

The three-day camping expeditions in Snowdonia after O-Levels were a highlight for several years. Fit rugby players would sneer at less athletic boys as they struggled under 30lb rucksacks for two days, but on Crib Goch, the tables were often turned. After the rucksacks had been left behind, the musclebound boys would sometimes freeze with fear and require coaxing along the ridge, while the nimble weeds took their chance to skip past them.

* * *

When an arboriculturalist friend of Keith Howard's visited The Coach House and explained to him how the *rhododendron ponticum* that produced the profuse, much admired blossom that arrived each June was actually killing the natural oak woodland, our mission became to eradicate it. It was hard work, but sawing down rhododendron bushes and lighting fires held a fascination for pupils (and some teachers); there was never a shortage of volunteers.

* * *

Being Warden of Farchynys for 16 years was a labour of love. I visited The Coach House about ten times a year, mainly with Geography field courses, walking and camping parties, decorating or rhododendron clearing parties. I never begrudged a minute: I was fully aware of the contribution Farchynys made to the education of pupils in the widest sense and to the life of the school. It was an immensely rewarding and enjoyable job. Long may Farchynys thrive!

Stuart Holtam: QM Staff 1972–2008; Warden 1979–1995; Head 1995-2008

Barmouth Bridge:
FRIED or BOILED?

When Benjamin Piercy built the viaduct in 1867 there was a man over at Barmouth who promised that if they ever finished it, he would eat the first train to come over. The morning it was due, a table was laid outside Barmouth Station with a starched white cloth and best silver and as the train approached, the chairman of the railway turned to this fellow and said, 'Here it comes now, do you want it fried or boiled, sir?'

The bridge, with its 113 timber spans and two of extended steel, opened to rail traffic on October 10th, 1867. Originally, it had a wooden lifting drawbridge to allow tall ships to pass beneath. In 1899, this was changed to the current swing arrangement. It was last opened in 1987.

An anecdote told to and quoted by Alexander Frater in _Stopping Train Britain_

A THESAURUS OF WEEKENDS

Arduous, arctic, desert, jungle and gothic;
Christian unionist, scouting, role-playing, outward bounding
Bikers and war gamers; cyclists and runners
Societies for Debating, History and Railways;
French immersion, German conversation
Parent cleaning [Editor's note: The Coach House, not the parents]

This is what they teach us

The weather – mainly rain

Farchynys and the weather are concepts often mentioned in the same sentence. As Graham Lightwood who, in March 1965, was one of the first Marians to experience Farchynys, put it, "The going on the whole was tough; we managed about 20 miles each day, mostly in pouring rain, drizzle, snow, sleet, fog and sunshine." Rain is, of course, the dominant feature of Farchynys' meteorological profile and is supported by Met Office statistics: The Mawddach area receives on average 1,000mm of rainfall per annum compared with Walsall's 725mm. As all weather experts know, the landscape near Farchynys is subject to orographic rainfall, produced as moist air lifts over mountainous areas near coastlines.

There's an old Welsh expression: "Glaw, fe ddaw fel y mynn," which translates into the English, "Rain comes as it does." And it does. The Farchynys duty logs are full of descriptions of how parties have had to contend with rain, mizzle and drizzle. For one Duke of Edinburgh expedition, it was, "the wettest day imaginable." One Master with a Year 7 group gave something of his mood away when he noted, "it always rains in Harlech." Other members of staff, almost as if in some musical refrain, describe returning to The Coach House "wet, cold and tired to dry out."

But the logs also reveal that serious meteorological adversity could bring out the best in Marians too. "Despite adverse conditions, the kids showed good morale and conviction," commented one master. Another reported how one Duke of Edinburgh Gold expedition was threatened when much of the UK had been put on red flood alerts, "but QM's lads carried on regardless." Teachers seem to be able to work their magic in even the most trying conditions. In the days of Arduous Training, Lieutenant Burgess's cups of extra-special "Home Brewed Tea" could apparently work wonders.

Moreover, it doesn't always rain at Farchynys and, as any frequent visitor will tell you, your stay can also be blessed with, "blue skies, and beautiful, beautiful sunshine." The log records a wonderful description by John Edlin:

"The Welsh countryside was at its most captivating. The sun low in the sky, lit the higher peaks with an even orange, while the valleys were almost blue-purple."

Mishaps, Emergencies, Disasters

And other challenges to morale

Blocked toilets – "How many degrees does it take to unblock a toilet?"

Cold showers

Ice Station Zebra conditions in The Coach House

Defunct cooking equipment

Fallen power lines so no electricity

Silver birch collapsing on the Cader Room

Flooding in the driveway

Midge bites

Lost in the wilderness (before mobile phones!)

Vomiting in the minibus – too much Barmouth candy floss

Motorbike yobbo attacks

Twisted ankles and a range of other medical predicaments

This is what they teach us

The advance party arrived at 21·00 hrs
preparation for Field Day and the
eekend. Members of the party included

EA

NTi

Cou

ſ

e

Duty Logs

One of the great treasures kept by the Wardens of Farchynys are the weathered leather-bound, A4 journals containing the handwritten accounts of group leaders' visits to The Coach House. Some are short and functional: details of date and time, of party numbers, the weather and a brief digest of activities. Others are extensive essays blending drama, wry observation and the gritty detail of endurance and leadership challenges. They not only provide a fascinating continuous log but also are a powerful medium for reinforcing the Farchynys grand narrative.

A personal favourite of the Editor's is taken from September, 1994, and channels the words of Julius Caesar:
  Venimus, vidimus, edimus, oravimus, dormivimus, egredi sumus.

A literal translation of this might be:
  We came, we saw, we ate, we prayed, we slept and we went.

Or perhaps rendered more poetically:
  Together we arrived and we observed; we ate, prayed and slept all together; we then went out into the world.

It is interesting to note that study is omitted from this particular list of actions.

ss
's
rvd

·s
rille

?, as
te.

rch

The Ventures spent the main part
the day in the hills, whilsr the
prepared for their activities which
to include bivouacing, backwoods

Mentioned in dispatches

The Farchynys duty logs are rich in little gems of banter in the exchanges between pupils and staff. At the ruins of Cymmer Abbey, one Fustie chipped-in "Why didn't they finish it, sir?" Young Marians are renowned for making real-time judgements and you can imagine the reaction in the minibus when one commented: "Oh sir, you've been overtaken by a Skoda." Meals were always a good spur for such exchanges. "What's the difference between beef sauce and non-beef sauce, sir?" and on a French immersion weekend, "la nourriture (sic) était bien et mauvais."

But members of staff knew what they had signed up for, and generally took it all in good part, and well knew that they would later pen their revenge, from the safety of the staff sitting room with a log fire and a glass of wine.

A special mention should also be made about the prefects who over the years have been much appreciated by members of staff for the crucial role as enforcers, occasional star chefs, and social shock-absorbers.

"Despite requests for small bags, H's case was as a big as him and B's required a double seat."

"A special mention for C who was virtually physically sick on smelling – let alone tasting – lasagne."

"A word on the little blighters: noisy, incessant but largely harmless."

"We had a test on how to use a toilet. Not all passed."

"One of the fifth formers was a diabetic and found it necessary to consume seven Mars Bars in one day in order to maintain blood sugar at an adequate level. It is a matter of debate whether the greater achievement lay in completing the walk or keeping down so many Mars Bars."

"Perhaps the most valuable lesson of the week is learning to wash up. Some of the novices have astonishing approaches. There is the fastidious hygiene freak who wants fresh water every three items washed. There is the 'I'm doing the washing up, but I'm not going to get my hands wet' genre, and there is the 'my watch is waterproof' brigade. But by the end of the week, they should be able to impress their parents with their blossoming new skills, if they admit to them."

Milestones

The Wrekin
Gateway to the border country.
Also a shorthand for
"going the long way round"
e.g. Mr Fink's route to Farchynys
via Bala

Breiddon Hill
An extinct volcanic hill in Powys

Welshpool
Home to a Tesco and The Welshpool
and Llanfair Railway

on the

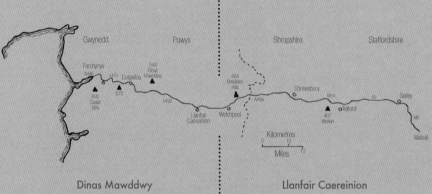

Dinas Mawddwy
The minibus
gear-change-challenge
on the Bwlch Oerddrws,
especially in the snow

Llanfair Caereinion
Locos in steam at the station

way

Dolgellau
"The meadow of hazels"

Farchynys postcode for Satnav

LL42 1TH

There's ore in them hills!

Tim Lawrence's CCF adventures

C ombined Cadet Force weekends at The Coach House began in the 1960s when John Dickson, John Anderson and David Pomeroy organised walking and camping expeditions known as Arduous Training. It soon became an Easter weekend fixture, with boys camping out unsupervised, and scouring local chapel inscriptions and phone box numbers as part of Wayside Pulpit, a message decoding activity we'd devised for them.

The Cadets' navigation skills were a little…inconsistent in those days. Infamously, one group once ignored their compass entirely, maintaining that the iron ore in the hills was distorting the reading!

"When a Cadet compared one particularly cold weekend to Arctic warfare training, the name stuck"

Steve Law took over the organisation of the course (by now renamed 'Adventurous Training' so as not to discourage less active Cadets) in the 1980s, introducing dry slope skiing to the programme of activities at nearby Bronaber.

The contingent was expanding and the RAF Section had begun to organise training weekends in the Autumn Term, taking in map reading around Llanfachreth, command tasks and field craft on the hill behind The Coach House. In the early 2000s, Bill O'Mara (The SSI – School Staff Instructor) set out a range which became known as O'Mara's Drift (perhaps influenced by the appearance of Rorke's Drift in the film *Zulu*).

These visits would often take place in December – one of the few times when The Coach House diary was free – but this did mean conditions could be challenging. When a Cadet compared one particularly cold weekend to Arctic warfare training, the name stuck.

As Arctic Warfare Training became popular, Antarctic Warfare was added in the Spring Term – with a similar syllabus aimed at RAF recruits. Later, Bob Champ and then Alex Hudson set up a similar weekend for Army recruits.

Desert Warfare arrived with the Gulf War – with airfields designed on the Estuary, and anti-tank berms (suspiciously like giant sandcastles) dug. In recent times, first aid, orienteering - and even jungle warfare - weekends have taken place. The Outward Bound weekend, currently run by Chris Larvin and Matt Rendu, has also become a regular September fixture with a full programme of hill walking. However, one of the most innovative has been Roger Machin's Command and Control battlefield simulation weekend where – operating entirely within The Coach House – orders are given in a war simulation exercise where Harlech is defended by Blue forces against Redland.

These weekends have always been popular and been filled with willing volunteers; indeed, a waiting list has often been in operation. It is my hope that they will continue for many years to come.

Tim Lawrence, Staff 1977–2014 and OC, CCF RAF Section 1997 to date

This is what they teach us

Cadair Idris
OUR MOUNTAIN

C adair Idris (also known as Cader Idris) dominates the Mawddach, its great 12-mile ridge standing impregnable to the south of The Coach House and viewed in full glory from the Gazebo. Cadair Idris (Idris' Chair) is the stuff of legend: it is said that anyone who spends a night on the summit wakes up next morning a poet or a madman. In 1860, a Dolgellau guide won a £10 wager by climbing the summit four times in one day. We do not know of this particular guide's bardic skills!

Contrary to popular opinion, Cadair is not the highest mountain in Merioneth; in fact it is only the 18th highest mountain in Wales, just failing to reach the magic 3,000 feet. It is, however, very old and consists mainly of Ordovician rocks shaped by volcanic ash, lavas and shales up to 460 million years ago.

Scouts and outward bounders know that there are three routes to the summit: The Pony Path from Ty Nant is easy but can take forever. Fox's from Lake Gwernan is more direct but the cliff scree can be dangerous on descent (how many party leaders have heard the plaintive words, "How long does this go on for, sir?"). The route from the south side starting at Minffordd actually involves two climbs and is the shortest and steepest.

Roger Redfern, the rambler and writer whose prose lit up the pages of *The Guardian* had family connections with people who owned a farm close to Farchynys. His family loved climbing Cadair and he noted how in his parents' day, "it was the done thing for walkers to reach the top of Cadair Idris by way of Barmouth Bridge, Arthog and so up to Llynau Cregennen before climbing to the watershed and traversing behind Tyrau Mawr to reach the summit of Pen-y-Gadair, the mountain's top." Redfern suggested that today's walkers are not quite as adventurous.

Arduous Training, July 1964
A seven-mile, 3,000ft climb up Cader Idris;
a 14 mile race around the estuary, and to
finish a four day hike in a diamond shape,
centred on The Coach House.

From Bala to the coast, 1992
"We were totally exhausted, particularly as we
had to carry E's rucksack, looped over a fence
pole for two miles. He was suffering from leg
cramp and could not have continued without
teamwork." Ian Cooksey

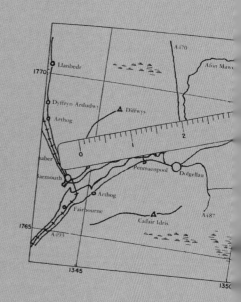

Year 7 Week punter feedback, 2016
"In the morning, we'd walk; in the
afternoon, we'd walk. Sometimes we
would walk all day."

This is what they teach us

"Without rugger buggers the trip was quite pleasant: only two or three bollockings. Good company and they seemed mildly interested in Geography."

[Editor's note: One month later, horror of horrors]:

"The worst fears were realised: rugger buggers. No concept of manners or thoughtfulness beyond their own adolescent pleasures."

"Probably the best group I've ever brought to do Outward Bound things. They ate everything, walked up, over and down everything and went to sleep when they should have; leaving the staff to indulge themselves in the traditional late night stilton and port fest."

"Perhaps we ought to swop-e-roony the spoony-woonies."

"The legendary arthritic knee."

"The famous Welsh mizzle had swept in."

The W_IT and W_IS_DO_M of Steve Law

In his own words, as found in the logs by the Editor

"This Biology field course was so small a group – we kept thinking we'd lost some."

"I think I know how the dinosaurs felt at the end of Cretaceous waiting for the end."
[Editor's note: Steve's comment on a final field course as Geology began to fade from the curriculum.]

"Cleaning tyrant: Mary Law; humble assistant, SJ Law."

"The ultimate dishwasher has arrived – me."
[Editor's note: the records show he refused to wash dishes with congealed porridge on them!]

"The bloody squirrel has bashed the bird feeder to bits. I'll beat the bugger yet."

"This is my last field course as a working man. I am available for consultancy and driving duties."
[Editor's note: The Warden's final appearance in this dramatic role.]

Faith, friendship and firm foundations

Peter Buckley and the Joint Christian Union

t was all down to Mrs Butt, an RE teacher at Queen Mary's, that I first joined the Christian Union on their annual Farchynys weekend. She was an old hand in taking parties of boys to Farchynys; I was just the new kid on the block. Over to you then, Mrs Butt – minibus driver, cook, speaker and recreational organiser…some woman.

*   *   *

That first weekend, we travelled to Dolgellau, and spotted a newspaper advertising board with the headline: "Dishcloth crisis." I remembering thinking, "Wow: the things that make the headlines in this part of the world!"

*   *   *

In the years that followed, Farchynys became a big part of my life. Once a year became twice a year for the senior Joint Christian Union and once a year for the Junior CU. I soon became the main organiser, taking on the role of chief-cook-and-bottle washer et al! As the years rolled by, the JCU numbers increased, until we were hosting one weekend trip and a four-day visit at Easter.

Farchynys became the place to go for the JCU-ers. Their Christian fellowship was prized among the young people from Queen Mary's Grammar and High School for Girls. Guest speakers came and made a vital contribution to the young people's understanding of the Bible. The pupils even formed a small band to accompany the singing – I soon learned to appreciate a more modern form of singing! On one of our visits, we had 44 visitors including staff – heady days.

*   *   *

I'm so thankful for the help of the many staff members who drove minibuses and organised recreational pursuits. Two of our teacher/drivers in particular made unforgettable contributions to our visits: one was caught speeding (not much over the limit, it must be said); the other put the wrong fuel in the tank of the minibus at a refuelling stop, causing us to grind to a halt on a traffic island!

*   *   *

My visits to this amazing place with the JCU will forever remain one of the highlights of my life. Farchynys' rolling hills and beautiful valleys hold a special place in the minds and memories of those who have had the privilege of visiting.

As with other visiting groups to Farchynys, many of our treasured memories are also tied to our reasons for being there. Faith was strengthened at Farchynys, the Bible more readily understood and relationships with other believers reinforced. Bonds and friendships were created that have held until this present day and, moreover, the foundations were set for many to find their calling in life.

Peter Buckley, Staff 1988–2012

"No boring Christianity here, we are alive and rejoicing in the living God. Lives have been changed in a wonderful way these last few days – many thanks to our speaker, Keith Rudman. The rain meant no football at Barmouth, but nothing could spoil this special weekend. I'm still smiling."

The Christian Union at The Coach House
Peter Buckley, QM Caretaker and Baptist Pastor, April 2003

This is what they teach us

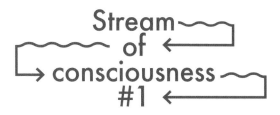

Stream of consciousness #1

Cadair Idris and scree slopes. **CCF Arduous Training weeks with 15-mile hikes via elephant grass from Penmaenpool to Pen-isa r-cwm and swimming in the river on arrival.** Dinas... going downhill in Stiffo's Moggie Minor at full speed in neutral and him shouting "Chwist! The brakes have failed!" about four fifths of the way down - he was joking, of course. **Fantastic open countryside and views over the Estuary which we Walsallians just didn't have. The closest thing for us was a trip up Barr Beacon.** Fools Gold ...Iron Pyrites. **Glorious red rhododendrons-in flower on entry to Farchynys.** John Dickson's Sunday roast. A whole onion was baked in the carcass of each chicken. **Knock-out table tennis with kitchen implements.** Phil Green fire alarms at 1 am, and "trail hunts" at night. **Making bivouacs on Headland as instructed by Sam Crudace, our veteran instructor.** Snowdon in icy, foggy weather. **The smell of vomit in the Bedford minibus - there was always one.** Mr Watson, French master (BBW) He had returned from living in Montpellier, and his English was a little rusty. Once, he bought 24 jars of mincemeat, instead of 24lbs of minced meat… you can imagine the effect on morale! **Old Boys' walking weekend, and ordering 32 cheese toasties from the sole barmaid in the pub.** The pure joy – much later – of being able to share the place with my wife and daughters.

Steve Parsons, QM 1968–1975

AN AU PAIR WRITES

13-15 Octobre, 1995

"I speak only French, but I try. Mon premier weekend anglais – lovely! Une campagne magnifique bien que ma préférence va pour la ville, mais le paysage reste impressionnant (so I do like the countryside!) The first time I go to the English beach? Cold! Sure, because I live in Cannes." Jessica – au pair in a party with the Parsons family.

Recollections of a long-distance runner

The Farchynys Run, a half marathon, began as Mike Jackson's initiative, many years before I arrived at the school in the 1990s.

It was held twice a year, usually in September and January, beginning at the lay-by at The Old Post Office in Bontddu. By the time I left QM in 2009, I had run it ten times; Philip Davies holds the record for the most staff participations and the fastest staff time. Other staff who took part over the years included Steve Law, David Isgrove and Bob Preese, as well as several parents.

In September 1997, on the day of Princess Diana's funeral, we opted to postpone the run out of respect until the following day. Instead we went out for a walk on the Saturday morning and Mike J offered up our own prayer.

The run came to an end in 2000 when the then Head of PE decided that younger pupils should not run half-marathons.

Mark Lawson, Staff 1991–2009

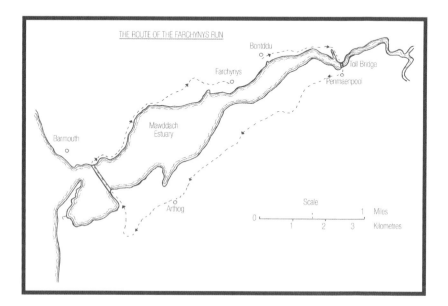

THE MARIAN

Marians on the Mawddach

The Great

This stamina challenging 46-mile ride began in 1983, when the first ever Marian *maillot jaune* went to Richard Baynham. The race was held annually until 1994, by which time 147 riders had taken part for a trophy donated by one of Farchynys' founding fathers, Jack Aspinall. Steve Law rode ten times on a variety of machines including the Oxidation-Powered Rust Mobile and a tandem, which he rode with the current Headmaster, completing the course in a very creditable two hours, 45 minutes.

Farchynys

Law also recorded a personal best of two hours 36 minutes on the 25th anniversary of the race in October 2008. "How can you refuse to go when, through the wind-and-pain generated tears, you can gaze at that magnificent landscape?" For those wishing to enjoy that glorious view over the rise at Harlech – sunlit beach and crystal clear peaks, it is important to consider one veteran's advisory: Insufficient Porridge Equals Cramp Syndrome!

Cycle Ride

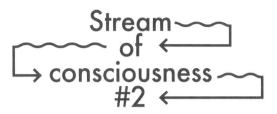

Stream of consciousness #2

Fustie Week 1998 (7E) - first time away from home with just friends, playing "run the gauntlet" in the dorms (on those brilliantly awful beds), getting to explore the woodland around the house and playing football on the estuary. A traditional childhood experience I'm glad to have shared. **Christian Union weekends – developing my faith, and my ability to talk to like-minded young people about a difficult subject in a safe environment… and dying my hair purple.** CCF (Signals weekend) – learning about old radios, sitting in the cold outside The Coach House peeling vegetables and developing a sense of discipline. **Brotherhood – going on CU and CCF weekends with my two brothers, developing lasting friendships and first experience of fraternity (after school, Freemasonry).** 'Traditional' upbringing – being outdoors and not in front of a screen, enjoying tradition and learning to feel (if with hindsight) part of something bigger than myself.

Nick Bridgman, QM 1998–2005

DOLGELLAU

Described in the 17th century as "a smoky Gomorrah of a place"; a town made with dark local stone and topped with dark local slate. The Marian, perhaps a somewhat confusing name to Queen Mary's folk, was once a great marketplace for wool, fleeces and minerals, and is now a car park, with Cadair providing a moody backdrop.

This is what they teach us

Barmouth
OUR TOWN

O r Bermo to those who know it well - and thanks to weekends at Farchynys, hundreds of Marians do. They come here to sunbathe or play footy on the sand-swept beach, to walk, run or cycle across its magnificent railway viaduct; to eat fish and chips at the Dolphin Fish Bar, to hang out in cafés like The Carousal (sic) or Davy Jones' Locker, to explore its cliff-hugging back streets ("The Rock") or just to spend their pocket money in its garish seaside emporia.

Barmouth is a town of paradoxes. Jessica Lofthouse, writing in 1970, said it was a town with a split personality: "part of it looks backwards to the day when it was the most secret of watering places," for the likes of Tennyson, Ruskin and Wordsworth who stayed in its elegant villas or Regency terraces. Whereas today, "the new Barmouth looks scruffy, soiled and tattered: a jumble of glossy granite and screaming plastic. "

Writing two decades later, Ian Skidmore was a little kinder in his judgement, thinking it "lovable rather than lovely." But looking beyond the superficial flotsam and jetsam visible in an old seaside town is that world-class scenery which, as Ward Lock judges, "so effectively combines the charms of the sea and the countryside." E Rosalie Jones, one of Barmouth's first historians, described the town's magnificent palette as, "the blue and purple hills, and the emerald and sapphire waves that forever toss their white foam upon the yellow sands they lap."

Is it then surprising that Barmouth with its beach, its bridge and its breeziness, continues to hold the warmest of places in Marian hearts?

Music on the Mawddach

Bev Wragg and the Chamber Choir

D uring the 1970s and '80s, the Chamber Choir used Farchynys as a base to perform concerts in the churches at Dolgellau and Barmouth. Both venues had excellent acoustics and it became a pleasure to sing in them; the proceeds of the performances were given to local charities through the churches involved.

This was the heyday of the Chamber Choir and, looking back, the content and standard achieved was truly remarkable.

The first concert was a great adventure. Sam Darby was a little reluctant, particularly when asked for the choir's return from Wales to be on Monday morning! He was, however, delighted by the local response to the concert and later quoted *The Walsall Observer's* observation that, "it was a very brave venture to take music to Wales!"

A weekend of rehearsals, run-throughs and occasional orienteering trips (organised by Ken Yates, who sang Bass) would culminate in the concerts, which always followed the Sunday evening services – a good way to get an audience. Many excellent soloists gave their time for free, as did organist Peter Morris, who played for all but the final concert on the list below.

The two December concert weekends were rather special in that they involved cooking Christmas Dinner for all; although in 1983 it was particularly manic. The meal followed on from a Joint Orchestra Concert, Full Choir *Messiah* performance in Walsall and was followed immediately on our return to the West Midlands with carol singing and the Joint Orchestra party!

The quality of the Duruflé and Fauré *Requiem* 1982 performance remains in my mind, along with the full church and the sight of Peter Morris climbing inside the organ to repair bits of it before we could begin. A repeat performance in Wolverhampton was attended by literally four men and a dog – Wolverhampton didn't know what it was missing!

Programmes were adventurous: Chris Rolinson, the composer and pianist, was a pupil in the Upper Sixth in 1976 when the choir sang his *Missa Brevis* in Dolgellau; 1983 was the only time we had a treble capable of singing the top Cs in the Allegri Miserere, and many a choral society would be hard pushed to tackle Kodaly's *Missa Brevis* and Britten's *Hymn to St Cecilia*.

14 Mar 1976	Various inc. Rolinson: Missa Brevis	St Mary's Church, Dolgellau
20 Mar 1977	Various including Britten: Hymn to St Cecilia	St Mary's Church, Dolgellau
10 Feb 1980	Byrd: 4 Part Mass/Monteverdi: Beatus Vir/Fauré: Requiem	St Mary's Church, Dolgellau
15 Mar 1981	Handel: Messiah Pts 2+3	St David's Church, Barmouth
14 Mar 1982	Duruflé: Requiem/Fauré: Requiem	St David's Church, Barmouth
7 May 1983	Britten: Missa Brevis/Lotti: Crucifixus/Allegri: Miserere/Rolinson: Missa Brevis/Kodaly: Missa Brevis	St David's Church, Barmouth
22 Dec 1983	Handel: Messiah	St David's Church, Barmouth
22 Dec 1984	Carols/Vivaldi: Gloria	St David's Church, Barmouth
25 Feb 1989	Handel: Messiah Choruses/Rutter: Requiem	St Mary's Church, Dolgellau

Perhaps one work that sticks in my mind was the Monteverdi *Beatus Vir*, not so much for its performance in the concert, but in The Coach House at supper on our return from the concert. The whole choir took part in an impromptu display whereby everyone stood up just to sing their part, often only a few notes long – and then sat down again: I thought this was bound to stop, but they continued with unbelievable enthusiasm until the end!

One of the organists at a later performance was Geoffrey Weaver, a friend of the Headmaster, Keith Howard, organist of Bradford Cathedral and, for the last 25 years or so, Conductor of Kidderminster Choral Society (with whom I now sing!). I told him of the Monteverdi performance and he was so impressed that he now uses the idea with choirs he conducts around the world.

These concerts – and many other musical expeditions – provided much enjoyment for pupils, visiting performers and local Welsh audiences alike, and helped to form links with the local communities. Long may the Welsh Centre continue to offer such opportunities to all.

Bev Wragg, Staff 1974-2007

The Coach House, the castles...and the secret nuclear bunker

History Society visits to Farchynys

John and Margaret Anderson pioneered History Society visits to The Coach House in the 1960s, creating a tradition that was to be vigorously maintained afterwards by Tom Perrett. To the great interest of the pupils, Tom complemented historical exposition with enthusiastic debate on current affairs with those members of the department who leaned rather more to the right of the political spectrum!

Between the late 1970s and 2014 weekend trips were organised by Tim Lawrence, assisted at various times by his wife Jenny, Rex Savin and David Rushworth. In the 1990s,

Lesley Horden from the Modern Languages Department joined in the weekends and has participated in nearly all of the 21st century visits.

Although the staff provided the leadership, the sixth form always took responsibility for the detail of the planning. Some generations took to this enthusiastically: in the 1980s, Mark Babington and James Champ insisted on taking responsibility for the shopping and catering. This degree of involvement was not sustained thereafter!

The venues visited differed from one weekend to another, but involved quite a lot of driving – and very often careful manoeuvring of the minibus. In the days of the roof rack, the risk of luggage disappearing in transit was a constant diversion. When the trailer was purchased, the challenge of reversing the vehicle down country lanes added a new dimension to the entertainment.

"Catering involved fish and chips at Barmouth on a Friday night – often in the pouring rain – and improvised buffets served from the door of the minibus at lunchtime."

Popular sites included Caernarfon Castle, Castell-y-Bere, Chirk Castle and Penhryn Castle, Plas Newydd, David Lloyd George's birthplace and the Marquess of Anglesey's Column. More obscure sites included Oswestry Hill Fort, Acton Burnell and Moreton Corbet Castles in Shropshire.

The cliff railways at Aberystwyth and – on the way home from Wales – Bridgnorth were also firm favourites. The secret nuclear bunker at Hack Green in Cheshire was a more esoteric location, and appealed to those interested in the Cold War.

Inevitably, catering involved fish and chips at Barmouth on a Friday night – often in the pouring rain – and improvised buffets served from the door of the minibus at lunchtime – often in laybys or car parks.

While writing this piece, I've looked through nearly 40 years of Green Books. Several hundred boys and girls participated and these trips were notable for the cooperation and good humour of the pupils. For many of us, these weekends will have a special place in our memories of Farchynys.

Tim Lawrence, Head of History 1995-2014, Head of Sixth Form 1997-2011, Assistant Head Teacher 2002-2012, Second Master 2009-2012

A Young Boy's First Visit to Farchynys

A song by David Hart

A weekend away, I'm glad to say
Is coming soon, this Friday afternoon.
The boys are excited and a little affrighted,
Leaving home behind, not knowing what they will find.

Mrs Watkins' spare dinners are always winners,
With shopping and packing, and nothing lacking,
Loading the minibus without any fuss,
Seeing what will stop and what must be on top.

Tearful mums and embarrassed sons say
"Please go, I'm fine." "Have a nice time.
Phone me if you can, if not me, your Nan."
"Please go, Mum, please go, I'm fine."

Loaded, as we go through town it's slow,
But now at last the journey can be fast
Thanks to 70 or more on the M54.
Then on the A5, Shrewsbury's endless islands we survive.

It was Welshpool's Milk Bar and supermarket Spar
That made the day, when we were half way.
They are memories now, those murals of cows,
And the secret drink packs hidden in our sacks.

The Welsh bends aren't easy and the boys are queasy,
But it's with delight that Cadair we see as we motor from Dinas Mawddwy.
That was Dolgellau we think, which is missed if you blink,
Then we are there, we are there, we are there.

This is what they teach us

Bunk beds and black bats in the rafters;
Spiders watch who sleeps on the bed where the draught is.
Senior boys making the laws which everybody ignores,
While the staff conjure up the finest cuisine that's ever been seen.

The meal devoured, a talk, then a tiring walk
With a run on the estuary sands and other fun
Before bedtime, and indeed, all is fine,
But nobody sleeps, nobody sleeps.

As day breaks, nobody wakes
Until the banging of bells and breakfast smells.
Barmouth for the day is what they say,
With rounders and cricket and sand and water play.

The sea is calm, the water is warm.
Then turning round we see the loveliest view to be found.
The fresh flat sand near at hand;
The church we find with rising rocks behind.

Our eyes look to Cadair Idris skirting the skies.
It is a world of wonder we sense
As the paintbrush of our imagination
Colours the canvas of our mind
In this moment of quiet beauty.

But the games go on, and it won't be long
Before we pack and leave and are back.
Let's say, there will be another weekend away
For us soon, leaving at noon on that day.

David Hart, Staff 1969–1999 and Programme Manager,
Duke of Edinburgh's Award

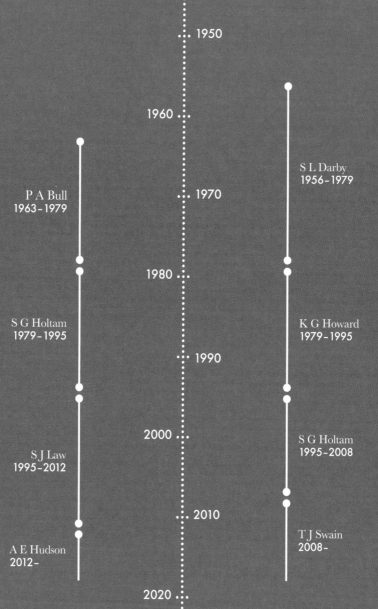

The
WARDENS

The
HEADMASTERS

1950

1960

S L Darby
1956–1979

P A Bull
1963–1979

1970

1980

S G Holtam
1979–1995

K G Howard
1979–1995

1990

S J Law
1995–2012

2000

S G Holtam
1995–2008

2010

A E Hudson
2012–

T J Swain
2008–

2020

This is what they teach us

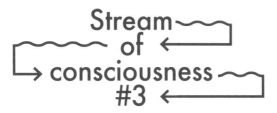

Stream of consciousness #3

Coffin lids. The bench seats along the window in the day room. Donated by a parental undertaker. **The Carousal Cafe – the wonderfully mis-spelt greasy spoon in Barmouth.** Dingbats (*pipstrellus tintannabulum* in our telling) the scariest sort of bat to be found out late at night when Fusties had no torches – perhaps in the Dingbat Cave. **Dolphin Fish Bar – Saturday night chip run, and official starting point of the Fastest Journey Home challenge – held for most of the time by John Anderson I believe.** Ferruginous Oxide – a dangerous substance found on the Headland. Also known as mud. **Fire drill – the cruelest of sports. PN Green, our Prefect, used to make us take off our shoes before running down the rickety fire escape and through the brambles.** Grey blankets. Often damp, usually crusted with toothpaste from late night tooth pasting sorties to nearby bunks. **Rommec - the old Commer minibus. Who would have to sit on the battery?**

Ian Trow QM 1971–1979

GERALDINE ACHIEVES AN UNUSUAL RECORD

"Breaking the habit of a lifetime, I felt compelled to put pen to paper to note the record journey achieved by Geraldine Brown – 11 hours from school to Farchynys. This was occasioned by:

1. An attack on the minibus by a motorbike thief wielding a woolly hat soaked in creosote

2. Two hours at a police station

3. A visit by GRB to every hospital in the Shrewsbury area to get a boy's eyes checked – luckily not damaged by the creosote

4. A car breakdown – and in the rain.

PS - We made the Midlands News." TFP 11 July 1988

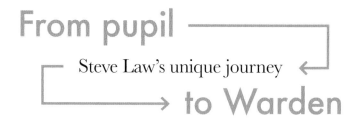

From pupil
Steve Law's unique journey
to Warden

I t took 30 years but it was worth it in the end. Chris Isaacs began it all in the autumn of '66, long before Fustie Weeks were invented. A small group of Scouts went up to Farchynys for the princely sum of £1.10s (or 30 bob). My memory is fairly vague, but I know we were told to follow a path up a stream to somewhere, and that we got lost and had to retrace our steps to get picked up.

Friday night's meal had been prepared by Frances Watkins's ladies of the school kitchen and consisted of big trays of meat pie, spuds, peas and carrots, gravy with stodge and custard for pud. Some of those trays are still in use at Farchynys today.

"I remember listening to the gulls, oystercatchers and a curlew, wondering whether I would ever return to such a tremendous area of beauty"

My other visits were spread thinly: because I played rugby and cricket, Dickie Cooper would rarely allow me to go. There was the infamous Dan Archer Scouting trip when Howard Walker got run over in Llanfachreth, though; and a Dickie Cooper rugby boys weekend which included an abortive ascent of Snowden when, hopelessly ill-equipped, we were beaten back by knee-deep snow.

Other trips came with Ken Yates on Biology weekends, with legendary snooker games in the Greasy Girdle (the Cors y Gedol hotel in Barmouth). These weekends with Ken brought it home to me what a wonderful place Farchynys was. I remember sitting alone on the end of the Headland listening to the gulls, oystercatchers and a curlew on my last visit, wondering whether I would ever return to such a tremendous area of beauty. That question was answered six years later.

*   *   *

My first Geography field course as a member of staff took place in September 1977. Sixth formers named Toussaint, Fitzpatrick and Wood were on that course; Fitzpatrick had cracked the first can of beer open before we'd reached the top of the school drive.

That was my first visit out of about 216 so far (an average of six visits a year for 36 years). I'm still going there in retirement, usually as chief cook-and-bottle washer on CCF weekends or as part of the leadership team on Adventurous Training weeks.

Until 1995, I was a leader or accompanier on various trips. I was always second-in-command (2IC) on Geography Field Courses, but on Geology weeks, I was leader. My 2ICs on those were many and varied: Roger Metcalfe, Neville Cooper, Lesley Horden, Carolyn Mellor, Stuart Holtam, Stuart Worrall, Julian Roderick and, of course, Ken.

*   *   *

At the same time that I was appointed Head of Geography and Geology, I was asked if I would like to take on the Wardenship of Farchynys. I had to think about that one over a weekend. I'm glad that I said yes.

Over the next 17 years as Warden, a number of changes to The Coach House took place. I felt that I couldn't be responsible for the many structural and essential maintenance tasks that were increasingly needed at Farchynys. These were handed over to a sub-committee chaired by Mr Keith MacFarlane. He was instrumental in persuading Headmaster Holtam to replace the roof, which led to its insulation and a makeover of the dormitory and staff bedrooms. All of the dorm bunks were replaced by a new design over one construction weekend when the bunks were assembled by a team of four, each of whom was given one task. After 11 bunks, we had become production-line experts.

The Coach House is less Spartan today but still has no Wi-Fi and few of the familiar trappings of life at home. The quality of life has improved for staff and pupils, but the isolation, quietness and darkness persist. Some may only visit once in their QM career, but there are still many who take every opportunity to be included in a party.

The ecological and landscape features of the surrounding countryside are as stunning as ever. Greater commercial opportunities exist for the visitor to this part of Wales nowadays, but there are still undiminished opportunities to seek solace and tranquility from the hurly burly of modern life. This is as true today as it was in 1966.

Steve Law, QM 1965-1977, Staff 1977-2012, Warden 1995-2012

3. Learning to pull together – the boys and girls remember

The Editor's first trip to Farchynys was in November 1968, on his 13th birthday. The trip is deeply etched on his brain, like the memories of these other Marians who came under the powerful influence of The Coach House on the Mawddach.

Damp, dark and dingy

Perfect prep for university digs!

'm almost sure I was in the first party of boys to go down to Farchynys after it was purchased by the school. We set off on Saturday, 23rd November, 1963, (a date fixed in the memory only because of President Kennedy's assassination the previous day).

Transport was provided in the form of an old van driven by Phil Bull, with the two masters in the front and the boys in the back. No seat belts, of course, but no health and safety issues either – though I do recall Phil cursing a driver in Lysways Street for not giving him the right-of-way when he was going up the hill.

Once we reached the house, we were marshalled straight into the kitchen to deposit the boxes of provisions for our stay. I remember it as damp, dark, and dingy, with the musty smell of a house that had not been used for some time - all in all, good preparation for university digs!

Our task for the weekend was to do some general tidying-up and sorting out, both inside and out. The weather was typically Welsh, a fine drizzle that never gave up, and added to the clamminess that pervaded the house. I can't remember us doing a lot in the way of outside work as a result, though everywhere was generally overgrown. Nor did we seem to do much in the house other than move things around and cook, but that was probably because Phil Bull was just using this as a dry run for future expeditions.

One of my tasks on the visit was to make breakfast on the Sunday morning: a fry-up. It was my first time cooking for so many, and it was difficult to keep everything hot, but it still seemed to go down well!

We returned to the West Midlands on Sunday afternoon. One of the boys on the minibus had a radio and, although reception was poor, we eventually found the Home Service and listened to such uplifting programmes as *Sing Something Simple* while the card school indulged in a game of brag.

*   *   *

I visited Farchynys several times more before I left school. I can't recall a time when the sun shone but I do remember that we were always allowed to slope off on Saturday nights in the sure and certain knowledge that we would find a pub – never acknowledged and never admitted, of course!

I don't think anyone ever actually managed to get drunk – either we couldn't afford to, or were challenged to provide proof that we weren't under-age (which, of course, we were).

Les Barnfield, QM 1959–1966

Coach House cuisine

50 years of food at Farchynys

O ne of the most obvious ways in which weekends at Farchynys mirror broader social change is in the area of food, both in its preparation and consumption. In the 1960s, as Mike Causer observes on page 68, caterers placed great emphasis on greasy, calorific diets as a means of sustaining the efforts of outward-bound adventurers.

The development of convenience foods and the arrival of a wave of international meal choices in the 1970s and 1980s, no doubt helped hard-pressed group leaders. Consider a typical weekend menu from 1986:

Friday	Saturday	Sunday
Oxtail soup.	Cream of chicken soup.	Pizza and chips.
Lamb chops, potatoes, peas, carrots.	Paella.	Instant Whip.
Sponge pudding and custard.	Viennetta and bananas stuffed with chocolate.	
	Cheese and biscuits.	

But it would be a major disservice to the number of great Marian cooks to assume that Farchynys food always consisted of unimaginative stodge and convenience foods. The Editor can still after all these years sniff the aroma of John Dickson's roast chicken, plated with squadrons of roast potatoes, or recall the first time he beheld Boeuf Stroganoff courtesy of Geoffrey Paxton, with his pears in burgundy wine to follow.

In November, 1992 Monsieur et Madame Swain presided over a Weekend Francais Gastronomique which featured wonderful apéritifs to sharpen a taste for ragoût de mouton à l'aubergine, salade de Ventoux and tarte aux pommes. Was it a jealous outward bounder, who facing less exciting fare the following weekend, looked back in the log and wrote on the Menu Gastronomique "and spam"? The following year, the First XV were treated to

Miss C Mellor's Khoresht Bademjan, a Persian lamb stew with aubergines, with homemade cheesecake for dessert.

There was an earlier occasion when the current Headmaster wrote about the highs and lows of catering at Farchynys:

"Every party has its finicky eater and a would-be chef faces limitations of time and money, but in a busy and tiring week, 20 empty plates can be a great source of satisfaction."

In more recent years, the increasing ethnic diversity of the school's roll has made catering for Farchynys weekends yet more challenging, as can be seen in these notes from the logs:

"Tea was lasagne, meat free lasagne, or vegetable lasagne plus salad, garlic bread and rice pudding to follow" and "Paul has performed wonders in the kitchen, catering for vegetarians, vegans, non-beef eaters and those who will eat anything."

On a recent Biology field course, dinner consisted of three roast chickens, two halal portions, four fish fingers and three Quorn sausages.

[Editor's note: The mention of Quorn at Farchynys brought him a brief moment of swaggering pride, as the launch of Quorn was one of the more memorable moments of his career in advertising.]

The School Song

"Floreat Reginae Schola Mariae"

Shout the motto boldly, for her sons are we,
Nurtured in her classrooms in our early youth,
Where we learn to cherish chivalry and truth;
Learn to pull together, each one with the rest,
Playing up and striving just to do his best.

*Chorus
This shall be our watchword, "Always play the game!"
Sound the old School's praises, trumpet forth her fame.
Though the seas divide us, we will not forget
That we all are brothers with a common debt.
Let us pay by giving, as we forge ahead,
Service to our living, honour to our dead.

This is what they teach us in the good old School;
"Only by obedience may we learn to rule.
If you fail, look closely, seek the reason why;
Strive and you will conquer, if you only try;
Strive, and bear in mind that each Queen Mary's son
Will rejoice and cheer you when the end is won."

Chorus   This shall be our watchword...

Present, Past and Future in one mighty whole,
Shining forth emblazoned on one muster roll;
When the call is sounded all must answer "Here!"
Voice and bearing showing neither shame nor fear;
Pointing to our honour, which untarnished stands
Bright as when we took it from our Founders' hands.

Chorus   This shall be our watchword...

Words: F.G. Layton Music: J.W. Ivimey

Learning to pull together

The Mawddach
OUR RIVER

T he Afon Mawddach has its source not far from the Cwm yr Allt-lwyd, a little north of Dduallt in wet boggy wilderness area far from the sea that was once described as a "belt of unremitting poverty," but which nevertheless became at Gwynfynydd, the hotspot of the 1860s gold rush. From there, the river joined by its tributaries flows down to Llanelltyd, close by the ruins of Cymmer Abbey, the dissolved Cistercian monastery and, to the west of Dolgellau, enters a wide and sandy estuary of great beauty: The best ten miles in Britain and, according to Rhys Davies, "a manifestation of divine handiwork."

At the mouth of this estuary stands Barmouth and its iconic railway bridge, which in October 2017 celebrates its 150th anniversary.

Yes, we canvas!

(or the shortcomings of CCF tents)

visited Farchynys two or three times between 1964 and 1967 with the CCF, always at Easter. From the fourth year, pupils had a choice between CCF, Scouts or cleaning the school windows. I was already a member of another Scout group and did not want to change allegiance, so the CCF it was.

I was already quite familiar with the Barmouth Estuary and its surrounds, both from Scout camps there and family holidays taken in Fairbourne. I had my own 1-inch and 25,000 maps of the area, boots, compass, and some understanding of weather in mountainous areas – I would happily take off for the day on my own, leaving my younger siblings behind. An extra week in Wales was certainly no hardship.

My recollection of first arriving at Farchynys was that there was one building in use and another that hadn't yet been refurbished. The accommodation was plain but no worse than the youth hostels that I had stayed in previously; the food likewise – although I understand others complained. In any case, it had to be better than Scout cooking over a wood fire.

At an Outward Bound course in 1969 I learned the reason for the greasiness. At the levels of exertion that hiking in the mountains requires, you need 4-5,000 calories a day. At the time such a diet comprised heavily of fats – today's more healthy regimes were unknown.

The week consisted of a few day trips, including an ascent of Cadair Idris of course – very boring when you got to the top [Editor's note: probably a minority opinion] – a three-day trip in the hills to the north of the Estuary, and a race around the Estuary crossing the two toll bridges at Barmouth and Penmaenpool. The race was the part I liked least, never having been a good runner, but somehow I put up a reasonable performance, perhaps to get it over with more quickly. We had to pay the tolls, of course. I recollect the Penmaenpool cost was a ha'penny.

The three day hike in the hills was much better, except for one thing. I was used to carrying Scout tents, which were nylon and reasonably light, but here we had the canvas CCF ones which were heavy, and had no fly-sheet or guy ropes. We were expected to find suitably-sized rocks wherever we camped and put them in pockets at the base of the tent walls. This meant that our choice of camp site had more to do with the presence of loose rocks than with protection from wind and rain. If a good wind did get up, the night was spent half-awake and holding down the tent.

There were usually patches of snow on the ground and it was normally lambing time so we'd often meet the farmers in their Land Rovers. Cooking was straightforward: Primus stoves and tinned Army rations. Navigation was easy for me and I strongly suspect that I made it clear to the others in the group. Streams would generally be full and very cold from the melting snow so getting wet up to the knees happened occasionally.

I have no photos of my visits, but I still do have my 25,000 map of the Estuary: "Reprinted with minor corrections 1960. Price: Paper- 5s. 6d. net".

Mike Causer QM 1960-1967

on minibuses

F rom the very first meeting of the QMGS Welsh Centre Management Committee in April 1963, transport was on the agenda. "Possible options to be explored for transferring parties to the Mawddach included by train, by hired bus or by school transport." Fairly immediately it became clear that a minibus was the only feasible option and looking into the capital cost of hiring, buying and insuring one became a key task of the Committee. After test drives of three alternative models, a Commer 14-seater with slatted seats became the favoured choice and was purchased for £836 3s 6d. Thus, did White-Knuckle Coachways come into existence.

As a valuable new asset, a standing order was passed that, "no boy in the school would be allowed to drive except in the event of absolute emergency." That didn't stop boys playing with the letters of the minibus and rebranding it as a Rommec. QM has owned many minibuses over 50 years and the White-Knuckle Coachways rides have become a defining part of the experience.

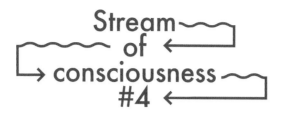

Stream of consciousness #4

On the clearance weekend I helped with, we carefully cut lots of rhododendron trees, dumped them in the old quarry and then realised we'd actually filled the quarry and had to cut them up all over again to retrieve and burn them. **I'm sure rhododendron burning gave rise to a fire engine call-out after the fire spread through the extensive root systems and appeared some distance away one night.** During some dorm games a future school captain was having a rough time and eventually yelled out "Ziggy!" at the top of his voice – only for Mr Holtam, the Warden before his rise to the headship, to appear and say, "You called?" **A Welsh 3,000 route with Mr Law where we never saw more than three feet ahead due to persistent rain and mist. He assured us we'd climbed them all.** The 1950s catering tub of Marmite – totally fine, as long as you avoided the rusty bits round the edges.

Peter Welch, QM 1982–1989

THREE BROTHERS, THREE HOTELS AND A FAMOUS INN

At the time when Marians started regular visits to the Estuary, there were three posh hotels that were run by a family called Hall. The dynasty was established by George and Nesta who handed their Cambrian properties on to their three sons: Peter owned the Gwernan Lake, Bill managed the Bontddu Hall ("one of the best positioned hotels in Wales") and John ran the Golden Lion Royal Hotel in Dolgellau where the Editor and his bride honeymooned in 1978. John also acquired the George III in Penmaenpool in 1964. John's daughter Gail was the last Hall in the business; she sold up in 1992.

Learning to pull together

Finding home, out in the field

I was at Queen Mary's between 1963 and 1970 and was therefore in the first generation to get to know Farchynys as a student. I went there on all manner of trips, from "bonding" weekends, form and Scout trips, to Geography and Geology fieldwork in later years.

I believe my first trip would have been in 1964. Perhaps on that trip, perhaps later (my memory does not go that far back) there was some kind of minor emergency – I vaguely recall that the teacher in charge had to take someone to hospital in the late afternoon to be patched up. As a consequence, a couple of us students were given the task of cooking the chicken for the 25 or so Marians. It was the first time any of us had cooked a chicken, but it turned out okay, and we didn't actually poison anyone.

My final trip was early in 1970 and, if it hadn't been for the rally-driver skills of Geography teacher Will Chipchase, I wouldn't be here today. After driving through flood water leaving Farchynys, the clutch on the school minibus went as we began our descent of Dinas Mawddwy. The sodden brakes did little to slow our progress, but we stayed on the road and finally rolled to a halt within walking distance of a closed-for-the-season youth hostel. The hostel manager kindly opened his doors and gave us a roof over our heads for the night, a local pub rustled up some dinner, and a near-disaster became a great adventure.

Fieldwork played a significant role in my later life, teaching in the UK, St. Kitts and Mexico. Later, it prompted me to start Mexico's first independent (i.e. not attached to a school or institution) fieldwork organisation for schools and colleges, which I ran for a decade. Following that, I became the Chief Examiner for Geography for the International Baccalaureate and was, for many years (until I passed on the reins last year) their Principal Moderator for Internal Assessment (Fieldwork).

School trips to Farchynys were certainly the catalyst for my belief that fieldwork should be an integral part of everyone's education. I offer my sincere thanks to all the parents and teachers who have helped make such trips possible and make Farchynys such a continued success.

Tony Burton, QM 1963–1970

[Editor's note: Tony still has the field sketch of the Estuary he created on a trip with Brian Edwards in June 1968; it can be found in its full glory on page 94]

Farchynys Hall

F archynys Hall was built in the 1870s by Thomas Oliver as a summer holiday home and appears to have been in constant use as such until after the end of First World War. The family fortune had been made from a cotton mill in Bollington located in the area known as the Happy Valley. The Oliver household, including governess and maids, would take the train from Macclesfield down to Penmaenpool and from there, travel by horse drawn coach to the Hall. The Hall was particularly popular with Thomas' son, Edmund (1866-1933), who encouraged family and houseguests to enjoy compulsory early morning swims in the Estuary. Edmund was also responsible for the introduction of rhododendron. Photographs survive of happy Oliver summers boating on the Estuary, paddling at the Boat House and taking tea on the Headland near the tennis pavilion. 1911 and 1921 were years of great sport on the Estuary's beats.

The family sold the estate in the 1930s to Mrs Morley who opened the Hall as a luxury bed and breakfast called Farchynys Mansion, which in its advertisements offered "faultless service, bedrooms with their own lavatories and running water." Other facilities offered included a tennis court, winter garden and a card room. Clearly catering for hunting and fishing types, Mrs Morley's country house also offered 600 acres of pigeon, wild duck and rabbit shooting. Since Mrs Morley sold up, the Hall has been a private residence (on several occasions), a boutique restaurant and more recently, holiday apartments available on Airbnb.

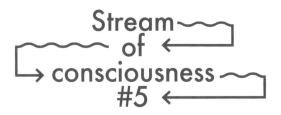

Stream of consciousness #5

Bonus of missing Friday afternoon lessons (in the first three years). **Buying the men's magazine, *Parade*, in Welshpool, then having it confiscated by Bill Chipchase - who knows what happened to it then?** Crafty fags down by the boathouse (but not for me). **Flapping canvas or rope on top of the minibus beating like a drum.** Ken Yates' custard – "one lump or two?" **Lighting a fire next to the slate bench on the Headland only to find it caused the bench to crack.** Lighting 'wind farts' in the dormitory darkness to the guffaws of everyone. **Looking for 'dingbats' in the dingbat cave.** Peeling what seemed like mountains of potatoes in a cramped steamy kitchen with blunt potato peelers. **Playing tag ping-pong in a circle, passing the bat to the next person until only two are left in.** Playing ping-pong and trying to hit the crack on the opponent's side of the net. **Shaking cans of fizzy drinks (for lunch) after a long walk so that they exploded everywhere - especially over faces and clothes - when pierced with an old fashioned can opener.** Sliding bunk springs down the telephone lines outside the dormitory window to see how far they went. **Spending all your money on tuck in Welshpool, then eating it before you even arrived at The Coach House.** Queasy winter journeys through winding and bumpy Welsh roads in the back of a hot damp minibus. **Tal-y-Llyn valley Geography field trips.** Trips to Harlech Castle with John Anderson, paying special note to the 'best' remaining medieval toilets in the UK. **Wishfully looking for gold in abandoned mines in order to get rich quick.**

Steve Bateman, QM 1967–1974

DINAS MAWDDWY

A gateway village to Snowdonia on the route from Welshpool to Dolgellau and the location of a sinewy mountain pass that has made many a Farchynys expedition just that little bit more exciting and memorable, especially in the winter. Dinas was occupied by bandits and robbers in the 16th century, known as the Gwylliad Cochion Mawddwy (The Red Bandits); they are celebrated today in the name of the local inn.

The Headland
OUR PLAYGROUND

Farchynys was purchased with ten acres of land that provided access to one of the prettiest bluffs and beaches on the entire Welsh coast. This immediately became a Marian playground for wide-games, football by torchlight, Cadet Force exercises or just chilling out in the Gazebo – which incidentally isn't actually a gazebo but which remains nevertheless one of the most popular slices of Farchynys life. First Warden Phil Bull called it one of the most majestic views in Britain. Blessed with wonderful views westward towards the bridge at Barmouth, but also subject to the full force of prevailing Atlantic winds, the Headland slopes down to mudflats and salt marshes where field biologists investigated dung beetles and footballers discovered the perils of quicksand soccer.

INITIAL MUTATIONS IN WELSH

One of the challenging aspects of learning Welsh is getting to grips with initial mutations, where under certain conditions, the initial consonants of words are altered.

The soft mutation

P>B   T>D   C>G   B>F   D>Dd   G>   Ll>L   Rh>R   M>F

gets
dropped

The nasal mutation

P>MH   T>NH   C>NGH   B>M   D>N   G>NG

The aspirate mutation

P>PH   T>TH   C>CH

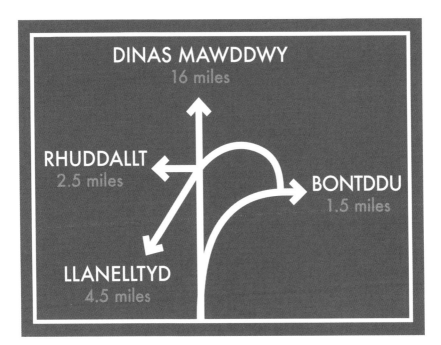

DINAS MAWDDWY
16 miles

RHUDDALLT
2.5 miles

BONTDDU
1.5 miles

LLANELLTYD
4.5 miles

Snowdonia

The Mawddach Estuary lies within the Snowdonia National Park, the United Kingdom's third National Park, established in 1951. In his *Shell Guide to the Mid West Wales*, Vyvyan Rees describes this landscape with a wonderful sense of poetry and colour:

"Walking in the high hills of Merioneth, the senses are assailed as sharply as the English Lake District. Cadair Idris and the Rhinogs all provide the small classical experiences: the smell of damp moss and the boggy places you are on before you can see them; the sheep tracks that seem so errant and vague, and yet add up to the shortest and on the whole, the driest route to wherever it is you are going; the white-rumped wheatears darting from rock to rock in front of you; the brace of grouse that suddenly breaks cover at your feet or the resentful croak of a raven that breaks the silence; the half supercilious, half-startled look of the sheep; the variety and closely integrated patterns of the short grass; the gnarled ancient look of the heather branches and their tough resistance to your step; the no-coloured and every-coloured rocks – purple, grey, beige, fawn, umber, sienna, green, mauve, blue – all lost in the pervading green and brown and purple of grass and heather, till you are suddenly upon them."

Workbooks

A fun way to discover and learn!

Fusties at Farkers
Year 7 weeks at Farchynys

The acquisition of Farchynys made certain that, despite the words of the school song, Marians were no longer only nurtured in the classroom. The Coach House on the Mawddach offered huge educational scope as a centre of adventure and learning in a contrasting setting, and nowhere has this been more evident than in the "Fustie Weeks" organised for all first years at the school.

Trips normally consist of a group of Year 7s, led by two members of staff, and usually assisted by two prefects. Parties spend five days at The Coach House, at the end of the summer term, working, playing and getting, as Alex Hudson, the current Warden, puts it, "to explore the world beyond Walsall."

The Fustie Week tradition goes back a long way. David Etherington, now eminent QC and bon viveur, was a prefect on a Ken Yates Biology Field Course in 1972 and remembers, "Each day, the boys, led by KIY and a walking stick, set off armed with all kinds of fiendish equipment, which appeared to consist largely of washing lines and bits of painted wood. One day was spent studying the distribution of organisms between high and low tide near the Boathouse."

The basic format has evolved over time but with the same focus on active outdoor learning. Philip Davies' contribution is a good case in point. Philip taught at QM from 1976 to 1992 and clearly loved Farchynys (he successfully completed 19 half marathons and still holds the staff record). Philip compiled and produced a series of worksheets – individual booklets completed by generations of boys in their Year 7 weeks.

David Rowley (QM 1979-1986), who is now a Geology and Geography teacher at Wells Cathedral School treasured his 1Z Workbook and kindly made it available for the preparation of this book. It's a wonderful artefact (you can see a selection of workbooks on page 79)

His assignments included rock pool micro-habitats on Shell Island, investigations at the Coed-y-Brenin Visitor Centre (where his field notes amongst the trees were judged as "rather untidy"), learning about military architecture at Dolwyddelan Castle, the mechanics of

slate quarrying in Blaenau and hydro-electric power in Ffestiniog. An exhausting week was completed by the conquest of Cadair via the Minffordd path and en route to the summit's Trig Point, the group discovered Llyn Cau and Mynydd Moel. On the way back down, his party were allowed to have, "a mega splash in mega-river." For his tremendous travel journal efforts describing the trials and satisfactions of the climb, David was told, "There's some useful stuff here, but keep it TIDY."

Over the years, Year 7 Weeks have included trips to local visitor attractions like The Centre for Alternative Technology (and games of "Spot the hippy"), Arthur's Labyrinth, Celtica, skiing at Trawsfynydd and Harlech Castle; expeditions to Merthyr Hill farm, slate skimming at the ever popular Blue Lake and outings to see Red Kites.

Fustie Weeks are deeply immersive experiences where young Marians not only learn about learning in a highly interactive way, but also learn about themselves, and the way they relate to their fellow classmates. Writing a number of years ago but with a message as relevant as ever, Philip Blackshaw (QM Staff 1989–2004) commented: "It's not the least of its advantages that the week at Farchynys for all first years gets them away from television and Nintendo Game Boys and forces them to adapt to the more taxing problems of living with people rather than screens, 24 hours day."

Eureka moment on the Headland!

I suppose the best memories of Farchynys for me are from the Biology field trip when I was in the first year of sixth form, circa 1974.

Chris Florkowski and I won the Biology prize for our treatise on discovering that a certain genus of slug was absent from one side of the Headland. It transpired that this side of the Headland had slow worms which were able to eat and digest this softer bodied slug more easily than other slug types, hence their absence. We replicated this work in the lab with a captured slow worm and a selection of slugs.

"When you are able to prove something, it's definitely a Eureka moment"

We analysed the soil and environmental conditions, comparing the two sides of the Headland to ascertain why slow worms were on one side and not the other. Sounds boring but when you are able to prove something, it's definitely a Eureka moment.

'Drac' Wiggin and 'Stiffo' Yates were the masters in charge on these visits. On one occasion, we went off on a trip to the sand dunes to do a vegetation survey by throwing a metre square frame over one's shoulder (to give the survey a degree of randomness) and listing the plants inside it when it landed. After lunch (sill in oil…revolting), we returned to the minibus only to learn that Stiffo had misplaced the keys. We tried to retrace our steps to locate them, but to no avail. Fortunately, Drac managed to open the window, break the steering lock and hot wire the vehicle into action.

We got back to Farchynys, Stiffo took off his boots and the keys miraculously appeared on the floor. They had dropped through a hole in his pocket and slid down the inside of his trousers! He had them about his person all the time! Naturally, he was in the dog house for a day or two…

Neil Boynton, QM 1968-1978

Taking flight at Farkers

I read Paul Brickhill's *The Dam Busters* when I was ten years old. From that moment on, all I wanted to be was a Royal Air Force Pilot.

The first time I flew in an aeroplane was three years later, in the back seat of a De Havilland Chipmunk, with 8 Air Experience Flight, RAF Shawbury, on the first day of a Queen Mary's Combined Cadet Force (C.C.F.) Long Field Day at Farchynys.

The next day we made our way to 'Freddy-Brown's' (Fridd-bryn-Côch, or 'Freddies' for short). Every so often, our march was punctuated by very loud jet noise, but no matter how much we scanned the skies, we could not see the jets. As we passed through the Rhinogs, we stopped for a rest. I lay on my back and gazed into the sky. A twinkle of light caught my attention – a Folland Gnat, doing aerobatics at about 20,000 feet. The distant roar of the engine rose and fell with the manoeuvres, and the jet looked so tiny in the vast blue vault of sky, as it wheeled and cavorted. I almost held my breath, afraid that a moment's inattention would cause me to lose sight of the tiny red and white arrow-head.

Later on, during another burst of deafening jet noise, I happened to look across the valley, and suddenly realised why we hadn't seen the source of the noise before. We were looking in the wrong place! The Gnat was flying so low that it was below the horizon, not in the blue sky at all. And it was going like the clappers! My ambition was utterly focused – having chugged along in a Chipmunk the day before, now I wanted to fly fast jets.

*   *   *

After various highs, lows and false starts, I was accepted for Pilot Training in the RAF I passed Basic Flying Training, and posted to RAF Valley in Anglesey, to complete my Advanced Flying Training on the BAE Hawk, the mount of The Red Arrows since 1980.

One of the irritating things about being a trainee pilot is that you have the most amazing experiences, but there's no way that you can share them with your family or friends. Your mates on the squadron aren't in the least bit impressed by your 'war stories' and the instructors have all been on the front line – try and impress them, if you dare! But on 7th December 1980, events conspired to nullify this irritation in the best way imaginable…

*   *   *

"I know that Wales is the shape that it looks on the map, because that morning, I saw all of it in one go"

The weather in North Wales in the autumn of 1980 was relentlessly bad. Eventually, the unusual step was taken to authorise weekend flying, in the hope that my course could get the required flying hours we needed by Graduation Day.

On the Saturday night, I telephoned Farkers, just to see who was there and was thrilled when the phone was answered by none other than Wing Commander John 'Dicko' Dickson, Classics Master and CO of QMCCF and my good friend Timbo Lawrence (History Master). "Get everyone on the Headland at 8am tomorrow," I told them. "I'll see you there!"

The next day, as my instructor, Adrian 'Bender' Benson, and I climbed up over North Wales, an incredible sight unfolded around us. I know that Wales is the shape that it's drawn on the map, because that morning, I saw all of it in one go. It was the only occasion that I ever flew in an utterly clear sky. From 35,000 feet, we could see Land's End and Carlisle at the same time, yet if we banked over to one side, we could see individual cars driving! The whole scene was overwhelming.

We levelled out at 5,000 feet above the hilltops, and I used the Mawddach Estuary as the line-feature for my aerobatics sequence which featured a Loop, Slow Roll, Lazy 8, Half-Cuban, Aileron Rolls, Derry Turns, and Roll-Off-the-Top (of a loop) Vertical Rolls, all conducted at about 450 knots, and between minus 2 and plus 6G. For once, every height and every entry speed was spot-on – the only time I had flown so accurately.

I'd told Bender about the CCF being there. When I'd finished my aerobatics, he put on full power and dived straight at The Farchynys Headland. As we roared over the Boat House at 550 knots and about 80 feet, I could actually recognise Dicko, standing there in his RAF raincoat, waving enthusiastically and surrounded by Cadets. Afterwards, others on the ground claimed that they could see me waving too.

Many years later, at the dinner to celebrate 100 years of QM CCF, I was accosted by guys whom I had never met before, who pumped my hand and declared, "Aggro Turner! You're a legend! I WAS THERE!"

Andrew Turner, QM 1970–1977

[Editor's Note: The Mawddach has a long history of being used as a training zone for RAF pilots. During the Second World War, when part of the Estuary was used as a practice area for D-Day landings, there were reports that a Spitfire flew under Barmouth Bridge. Today, jet spotting appears to be a very popular pastime and a local B&B run by Mr and Mrs Finch at Farchynys Farm does very well accommodating these enthusiasts.]

John Ruskin was the writer, critic and artist who helped to define the public taste of Victorian Britain. A polymath and keen student of geology, he loved scenery, especially the Mawddach Estuary:

"There is no better walk than from Barmouth to Dolgellau other than from Dolgellau to Barmouth."

"Old Cader is a grand fellow and shows himself superbly with ever changing light. Do come and see him."

Charles Darwin writing to Sir Joseph Hooker in 1869.

A Gothic weekend

Farchynys early acquired a reputation for austerity. As *The Marian* noted in 1965, "A weekend at Farchynys is to a large extent getting by without it; 'it' being some of the luxuries of home and the delights of Babylon." But I wonder what that writer would have made of the spectacular Gothic experiences shared by A- level English students at The Coach House in an appropriately spooky November 2011?

Taking the long view, Gothic experiences are nothing new on the Mawddach. In the early nineteenth century, the area was popular with many writers and artists. Samuel Taylor Coleridge climbed Cadair, Percy Bysshe Shelley visited in 1812 and, perhaps inspired by this, our latter day Goths were a party of A-level sixth formers intent on days of, "exploration and transgression" as one of them recorded. A suitably sybaritic and uncanny programme included readings of Horace Walpole's *The Castle of Otranto* and Marlowe's *Dr Faustus* in The Coach House, of *Dracula* in the Gazebo by torchlight served with popcorn and a performance of *The Woman in Black* in the suitably ghostly atmosphere of the Church of St. Mary and St. Bodfan, Llanber.

WIN-WIN WEEKENDS

"A great time was had by all. The boys enjoyed it enormously, and so did we. There were lots of comedy moments and memories to take away. Long live Farchynys!" SMT First Year Week 4

No! We can't find our BANANAS!

I have many fond memories of Farchynys: It offered golden opportunities for self-development. For some pupils, it was probably the first time that they'd been away from home without their parents. First-timers were often horrified to discover they were on a cooking, washing up and cleaning rota: on more than one occasion I had to console a fellow pupil, almost in tears at the sight of a massive pile of washing-up.

The setting was – and still is – utterly beautiful. Rain or shine, I loved walking down past the mysteriously derelict tennis court to the beach to skim stones into the Estuary.

My first visit was with Peter Bishop, a fellow first-former and our Latin master John 'Dicko' Dickson, who was organising a sixth form archaeology trip.

The archaeology bit was complete fiction – I guess the teachers have to provide some sort of plan – and it turned out to be more of a 60s music-fest: *Sergeant Pepper* had just been released and we had a large dose of that. I got pretty good at table tennis. A damn good time was had by all, and we needn't bother too much with the details.

Then there was the Bonfire Night weekend. I don't recall who was there or who the supervising teachers were, but the latter went off to the pub in Barmouth on Saturday night, leaving us to amuse ourselves. Innocently, I'd packed my rucksack with spare clothes, toothbrush and soap; everyone else had filled theirs with super-bangers and rockets.

We formed two teams: those in the house and those outside. Then hell was unleashed. Bangers were lit and thrown by the dozen. Rockets were launched from lengths of bamboo at shoulder height. Most of the windows were open and, when an ordnance landed in the dormitory, fuse fizzing, we were faced with the dilemma of whether to it back outside, or accept inevitable explosion.

The effect was truly spectacular – no firework display I have been to since has come close. Amazingly, the masters didn't notice the stench of gunpowder and the cloud of smoke that lingered over the place for hours afterwards. (I probably should add that no boys were physically harmed).

* * *

Dan Archer was master-in-charge on another weekend I spent with a fellow sixth-former (Howard Walker), and a group of Fusties. It was an opportunity for the new boys to go to Farchynys for the first time. A great trip, with gorgeous weather and long evenings mucking about on the beach and walking over the headland.

One evening, Howard, Dan, another teacher and I were discussing what we might do after supper. We were all enjoying that masterpiece of desserts, bananas and custard (I was particularly smug as my custard was utterly lump-less – no easy task when catering quantities are large).

We thought a game outside would be good and someone suggested a paper chase. I happened to be eyeing the huge pile of banana skins and was struck by the brilliant idea that we could use these instead of paper.

Howard and I prepared a tricky route, leaving a trail of banana skins across the Headland. Then we released the boys in groups of three or four and waited. And waited. And waited.

What hadn't occurred to us was the fact that when bananas are left on the ground, they go brown and become rather difficult to see. And now the sun was going down and the Headland, with its dense tree cover, was becoming a dark and somewhat spooky place…

Soon, we had about ten smallish boys lost in the dark and the game had turned into a challenging search and rescue scenario. It was a couple of hours before we had finally rounded up the last boy.

I realise now that what Farchynys taught me most of all, was never to lay a paper trail with banana skins: and that's a lesson I have followed to this day!

Andrew Elliott, QM 1966–1973

A voyage of self-discovery

During my time at QMGS, and subsequently as an Old Boy helping out with CCF Adventurous Training at Easter 1993, I was fortunate to have stayed at the Farchynys Coach House on many occasions. It was a great privilege, for which I'll always be grateful – especially to the staff whose energy, enthusiasm and commitment made Farchynys the institution that it is.

From that first week-long introduction as a 12-year-old boy to my final stay as a young man, I relished every aspect of my visits. It started with the anticipation and excitement in the days beforehand, then with the chaos of loading luggage and kit onto the minibus. The journey itself would pass with all of the attendant wise-cracking and dicking-around to be expected of a busload of teenagers, and with the welcome ritual of stopping to refuel and refresh at Welshpool.

Journey's end approached with the left turn off the A496, and the slow dark ascent up the stony driveway past Farchynys Hall to The Coach House, followed by the omnishambles of the de-bus and unloading of luggage. Then there would be that first intake of the cool, damp woodland air of the Mawddach Estuary, so very far removed from that of the Black Country, and after that, the race to the dormitory to secure a preferred bunk, the posting of rotas, the reading of safety and fire regulations, and the slow restoration of some semblance of order and calm before dinner, table tennis, and bed. Regardless of why you were there and when, these conventions remain timeless.

I have many fond memories of Farchynys: of the staff and fellow pupils, some of whom would go on to become lifelong friends; of trips to Barmouth; of antics in the day room and the dormitory; and of the exhilaration of late night escapes down the fire escape and out into the woods of the Headland by torchlight. But my fondest memories are probably the days and nights I spent walking and camping out on the Rhinogs, the Arans, Diffwys and Cadair Idris: the great sense of space (in such sharp relief to the urban West Midlands) and the physical challenges of the routes across arguably the oldest and most rugged range in Wales in often harsh weather conditions. With the great sense of freedom I experienced, there came also a growing sense of personal responsibility, of trust, self-belief and a concern for the safety and wellbeing of others.

"That first intake of the cool, damp woodland air of the Mawddach Estuary, so very far removed from that of the Black Country"

For me, it's probably in this latter respect that Farchynys can continue to lend itself most effectively to the personal development of young people. By removing them from the strict routine of the classroom environment and transporting them instead to this remarkably wild and beautiful landscape, pupils are afforded a very special opportunity to develop the sort of self-reliance, confidence and team-working that is only really ever achieved through new experiences and self-discovery.

Matt Killian, QM 1984–1991

The search for lost Roman roads

I t began one night in Autumn Term at John Anderson's flat in Lichfield Street looking at old maps. The quest soon took us to the desolate old fort at Tomen y Mur near Llyn Trawsfynydd and finally to the frozen hills of the Nannau estate at Brithdir. We were looking for the road that connected a network of forts that was used by the Romans to secure their supply lines and the Empire's western frontier.

Throughout the 70s, there had been significant local resistance to Roman rule and the Ordovices had massacred an entire regiment of cavalry. In AD 78, the celebrated general Agricola was appointed Governor of Britannia and one of his first priorities was to finish the conquest of Wales. Tacitus tells us he quickly exterminated the Ordovices, and then struck north to the island of Môn where the Druids were rounded up and the inhabitants forced to sue for peace.

Sadly, through the mists of time, the Editor cannot say with any certainty if his search was ultimately successful, but he can attest to the quality of John Alwyn Dickson's roast chicken dinner that was the highlight of a second visit to find the lost legions of Rome.

War of the Rhodies

Victorian and Edwardian industrialists who wanted a quick result in prettying up their newly acquired baronial landscapes brought in an exotic shrub called *rhododendron ponticum*. With evergreen leaves and violet/purple flowers, the rhododendron quickly colonises and begins to crowd out the natural flora, especially that found in oak woods. Once established, the shrub is notoriously difficult to eradicate as its roots easily create new shoots. By the time of Stuart Holtam's wardenship (1979–1995) the Rhodies on the Farchynys Headland had become a serious problem and SGH was equally focused on their extermination.

The Editor can personally attest to this when, at some QMC event, the Warden Stuart Holtam persuaded him to cough up £75 for a mobile root treatment spraying kit. He got off lightly, as Stuart was just as tireless in recruiting warriors to address the issue in hand-to-hand combat. Father-and-son weekends were held (what great marketing, Stuart!): "We came, we sawed, we got tired," wrote one parent. Bill Cheesewright brought a chainsaw and a camcorder: after all these were different days for health and safety. Peter Welch, with appropriate classical imagery wrote, "Bleary eyed, we returned to Hades and the fires of Hell."

By the time Stuart had assumed supreme power as Headmaster, the War against the Rhodies had been won and he was able to report that our headland no longer resembled the Himalayas.

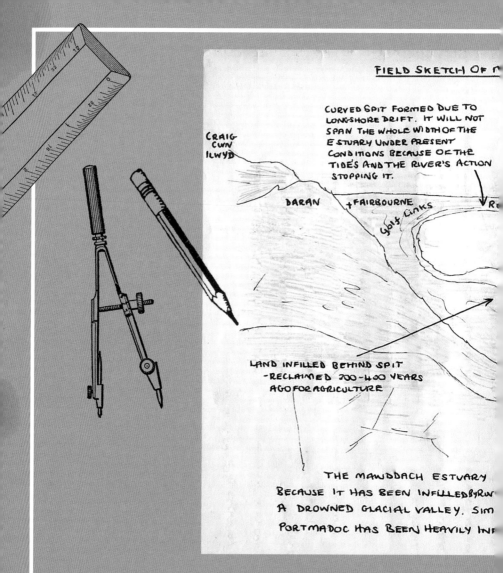

FIELD SKETCH OF M

CRAIG CWN ILWYD

DARAN

CURVED SPIT FORMED DUE TO LONGSHORE DRIFT. IT WILL NOT SPAN THE WHOLE WIDTH OF THE ESTUARY UNDER PRESENT CONDITIONS BECAUSE OF THE TIDE'S AND THE RIVER'S ACTION STOPPING IT.

+FAIRBOURNE
Golf Links

R

LAND INFILLED BEHIND SPIT -RECLAIMED 200-400 YEARS AGO FOR AGRICULTURE

THE MAWDDACH ESTUARY BECAUSE IT HAS BEEN INFILLED BY RIV A DROWNED GLACIAL VALLEY. SIM PORTMADOC HAS BEEN HEAVILY INF

Forming ambition

Tony Burton's 1968 sketch of the Mawddach Estuary: early evidence of a life in the field. Tony is the author of: Western Mexico, A Traveler's Treasury (4th edition, 2013) Lake Chapala Through the Ages: An Anthology of Travellers' Tales (2008) and co-author of: Geo-Mexico, The Geography and Dynamics of Modern Mexico (2010).

ESTUARY

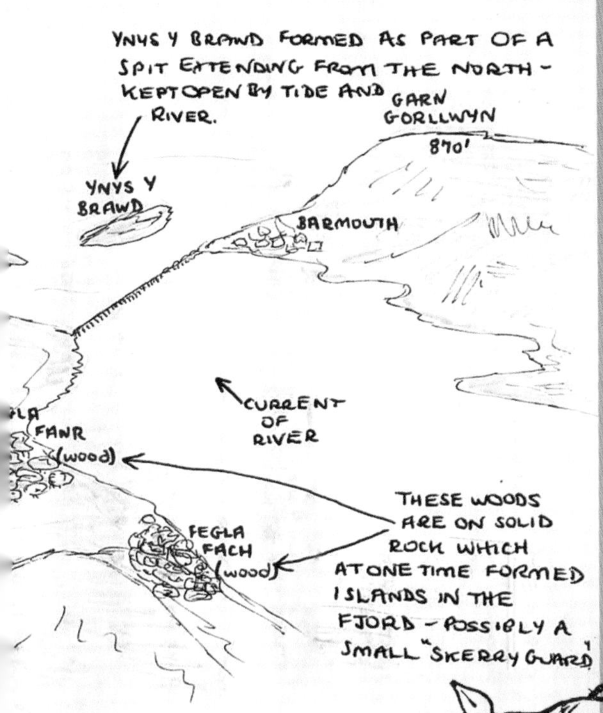

YNYS Y BRAWD FORMED AS PART OF A
SPIT EXTENDING FROM THE NORTH -
KEPT OPEN BY TIDE AND
RIVER.

GARN
GORLLWYN
870'

YNYS Y
BRAWD

BARMOUTH

CURRENT
OF
RIVER

...LA
FANR
(WOOD)
...ED

FEGLA
FACH
(WOOD)

THESE WOODS
ARE ON SOLID
ROCK WHICH
AT ONE TIME FORMED
ISLANDS IN THE
FJORD - POSSIBLY A
SMALL "SKERRY GUARD"

...ERY CHARACTERISTIC FJORD. THIS IS
...VE SAND AND ALLUVIUM. IT IS, HOWEVER,
...THER NORTH, THE GLACIAL VALLEY AT

New windows on the Mawddach

Headmaster Timothy Swain introduces the Farchynys Estate

Barn and Cottage have entered the Marian Lexicon alongside Coach House: three properties making up what we are calling the Farchynys Estate. Pretentious? Perhaps a little, but I prefer to see a healthy pride (as well as huge affection) for the achievements of the school community and it has been a team effort securing Mr Darby's Hahn-inspired legacy. It has required vision and decision, resilience and resourcefulness, hard work and hard cash; but above all it has demanded collaboration – a joint effort towards a common goal. For us, there is no hollow ring to the slogan "stronger together."

The Estate not only safeguards our Marian traditions on the Mawddach, but also prompts us to imagine new opportunities. With The Barn's space for work, seminars and conferences and the family-friendly accommodation in The Cottage, we now have a centre that we can more readily offer to others. Private lettings will secure revenue to finance the project in times of swingeing cuts to education budgets, but more exciting is the prospect of allowing other groups to share the privileges we have enjoyed for half a century. Expertise acquired over decades (in putting on Geography and Biology field courses, for example) can be marketed to other schools. All it needs is a bit of Marian enterprise.

Some may worry about letting others use Farchynys, but my hope is that some familiar words will underpin the next chapter of Marians on the Mawddach, words that are in our DNA. It is surely by giving it generously to others, that we will secure our Welsh wealth for the future.

The Farchynys Estate

The Coach House
purchased 1963

The Extension
built 1974

The Barn and Cottage
aquired 2017

Here come the girls

One of the most important social changes to weekends at The Coach House in the noughties was the regular appearance of girls – initially QMHS pupils joining Christian Union trips to Farchynys; shortly after, a part of expeditions as fully fledged members of QMGS Sixth Form.

Claire, a former Head Girl of the High School wrote in the Duty Log, "I left QMHS two years ago and still keep coming to Farchynys to avoid losing touch with Queen Mary's completely and because I love the charm of the place."

Drinking (tea) for England

S uch an amazing weekend with just the eight of us. We all had the chance to learn how to mountain bike. We ranged from novices to a professional biker! On the Sunday we went to Barmouth to watch the dirt biking, followed by tea and scones (How posh!).

There was a nice landslide from Ms Roberts-Gawen, deciding that she had to injure both sides of her body so that neither side felt left out. Abi decided to fly over her handle-bars, followed by a well-executed landing! Tara and Emily were the only two to not fall off their bikes and managed to complete the dangerous 'Red' course. Both girls succeeded in flying over the jumps and landing perfectly without stumbling. Along with Mr Clements, Kathryn decided to take a break due to cramps making her unable to walk.

The food was delicious and Tara and Abi managed to steal half of Mr Clements' cake and drink enough tea for England! We discovered Mr Lax has an obsession with cheese and Ms Roberts-Gawen likes to have reconstruction! **[Editor's note: I quite understand the need for "reconstruction" following such injuries in the line of duty]**

Emily Pitt, Senior Prefect, on the first ever girls' mountain biking weekend

A chance
to breathe

visited Farchynys four times whilst at school. Three of these trips were with the History Society, led by Tim Lawrence and Lesley Horden. The other occasion was as a helper at the open day for Fusties. I have been back since as a student at Oxford.

History Society trips were a lot like my family holidays in the UK – driving long distances around different bits of the country, popping into attractions, particularly National Trust properties, and eating picnics out the back of the van. I was quite surprised that a school trip could be so much like a wacky Taylor family holiday!

For me, Farchynys was an escape. School days were long and tiring and it was great to think that at the end of the week you could get away from it all and head up to North Wales for something non-academic with friends, as well as with kids from other classes who didn't have the same work as you. In my second and final year at QM there was a lot more pressure and greater difficulties at school; being able to get away became even more valuable.

A weekend at Farchynys probably meant cramming in some work late in an evening (especially Lloyd Taylor's History notes) but it was always something to look forward to at the end of a hectic week, when maybe every lunch had been taken up by some meeting or activity, or the bus to school had been late every day! Friday lunch would mean a change of clothes and fish and chips to look forward to in Barmouth and the promise of relief from school claustrophobia.

Of course at QM, there weren't many girls, which marked us out quite a bit. At the time, there wasn't any separate girls' accommodation at Farchynys, so I had to sleep on a camp bed in the Cadair Idris room. Sleeping in makeshift accommodation away from the others in the party definitely said something about being a girl at QM! `

I remember waking up in that cold classroom every morning to alarmingly bright sunlight – there weren't any curtains so, no matter the weather, the sun always came streaming in. It was a sensation unlike any I've experienced anywhere else, but one that I always remember when I wake up in a tent.

I have brought my other half to Farchynys and taken him on a trip not too dissimilar

from our History Society expeditions. Being able to show him The Coach House and return as an adult genuinely meant a lot to me. I go on about Farchynys, so sharing it 'in the flesh' was great – a happy memory that now has a welcome place in a different part of my life.

Farchynys is at the top of the list of things when it comes to comparing QM with the fee-paying schools that many of my peers at Oxford went to. At Oxford, I have developed a bit of a chip on my shoulder about private schooling and Farchynys is always there when I'm speaking up for QM and grammar schools in general. Tim Swain often talked about the virtue of QM as a free school for Walsall by foundation and I never appreciated the potential threat of non-free schooling behind that claim. I do now, and Farchynys is a major plus point for QM and what it stands for.

Roxanne Taylor, QM 2011–2013

[Editor's note: The renovation work since 2011 has made conditions for women at The Coach House far more comfortable than on Roxanne's first stay.]

The point of Farchynys

actually won an award for the most use of Farchynys – some would say it's because I wasn't going to win an award for anything else... but I really enjoyed the freedom and adventure that we gained and looked forward to that Friday afternoon ritual of loading the roof rack on the minibus. The breadth of opportunity that having a base in such a superb location was reflected in the range of clubs and societies that used it. For me personally that ranged from Gold Duke of Edinburgh expeditions and rhododendron clearance to Geology trips, where I found a trilobite that shouldn't have been in the geological formation where we found it, and the satisfaction gained in it being sent to a museum. A place to find yourself, which for me, led to a lifelong interest in outdoor spaces and the mountains of North Wales."

Peter Welch QM 1982–1989

Welshpool – are we there yet?

n the early days of trips to Farchynys, before the M54 was finally completed in 1983, the journey from Walsall to Farchynys could take at least three and half hours, at first on slatted seats, so a pit-stop and a leg stretch was essential. Welshpool, or as it is known in Welsh, Y Trallwng, lies on marshes near the Severn just over the border and is the perfect place to refuel. Its High Street soon became a popular haunt of the minibus and its Marian passengers searching out morale boosting supplies.

For some years, one of the most sought after emporia was Langford's, purveyors of pies and sausages which fed and raised the spirits of many a Marian on the Mawddach. Sadly, Langford's passed its sell-by date a few years back, so depriving new generations of Marians the opportunity to savour one of Welshpool's more Proustian delights.

BIOLOGY FIELD COURSE
2005 DRAMATIS PERSONAE

Legends
Wasters
Geeks
Team Gingers
Fairy Cakes
Jug Eared Wonders
Cousin-Took-Entrance-Exam
He-Actually-Speaks
Table Tennis King
Blood Donor
Token Bird

4. Present, Past and Future

Since the first convoy turned off the Barmouth road and up the driveway, there have been many changes to the Farchynys experience, largely reflecting the profound social change that has taken place since Sam Darby and co made The Coach House project a reality.

Three heads; three wardens

Themes for visits have constantly morphed over the years. The CCF's Desert and Jungle warfare weekends reveal Britain's new military priorities following the end of the Cold War and even more contemporary conflicts.

Mixed gender groups have become more frequent and with the advent of Queen Mary's joining the Mercian Academy Trust, will become even more so. The improvisation and field modifications undertaken by the first female guests will become part of the Farchynys folklore, but increasingly not the current reality.

Health and safety has also become a much more evident concern and necessary process over the years. This has placed even more responsibility on the shoulders of staff and group leaders. For a Welsh Centre whose raison d'être is the experience of adventure with at least some controlled element of subjective danger, this has posed some interesting questions. One master confided to the duty log the difficulties of running an Adventurous Training Week "without adventure".

But to think that expeditions to Farchynys have gone soft would be very wide of the mark. Boys and girls still take responsibility for planning significant hikes over the hills without direct staff input. They are still climbing Cadair in the rain and facing other challenges the Mawddach weather brings.

Indeed, while there has been some significant change since 1963, it is striking how much continuity there is. The cost of a weekend is one simple indicator: in 1963, the cost

The Editor with current Year 12s and Year 7s

was set at £1.25 or more precisely at the time, 25 shillings; in June 2016, this was £55, which is about the same at constant prices. Continuity is also evident in the narrative that is told: the banter between pupils and staff; the games of footy on the beach; throwing up and cleaning up; the evening stroll to watch a mesmerising sunset at the Gazebo; the late night conversations in the dorm and the inevitable falling asleep in the minibus on the way home. These things provide powerful connections between Marians-past and Marians-present.

For a school with a great academic tradition like Queen Mary's, Farchynys provides a contrasting and inspiring setting for learning opportunities. Colin Mortlock, the author of *Adventure Education* (written in 1978 and reflecting the Hahn tradition) concluded his practical guide for schools with this thought:

"Education should equip an adolescent for living in the broadest sense, as a responsible member of society, as well as giving him the skills with which to do a job. Before he can live in this sense, he needs to become fully aware of his own abilities, and have found self-confidence and self-respect."

Today, while some of Hahn's philosophy is not without its critics, his influence on outdoor educators remains strong. Sean Hewlett is one of the senior leaders at Yenworthy Lodge in North Somerset, the outdoor centre of Oxfordshire County Council and he shared with the Editor what he considers to be the main benefits of his centre's 'week- away' courses:

- Stronger relationships and new friendships
- A chance to self-reflect upon a student's place in the group
- Confidence in some areas of physical ability

- New skills acquisition
- Stronger relationships with teachers: adults seen as "fallible" human beings, some of whom are actually good cooks!

Sean also notes how the teachers he meets at Yenworthy are able to build better relationships with their pupils and can profit from the chance to see them "in the round." But if the value of adventure education is well appreciated, its financing is now becoming a serious issue. In this regard, Queen Mary's is very lucky to have use of an asset like Farchynys.

Current QM pupils we spoke to would agree with the thrust of Sean's ideas. Consider the maturity of these reflections from a group of current Year 12s:

"Farchynys gives you a well grounded perspective on the outside world."

"Farchynys was a great way to build my confidence and put myself out there."

"We wouldn't be as good friends as we are now had it not been for Farchynys."

"Farchynys is one of the special things the school has."

"Farchynys is one of the things I'm going to miss most about QM. To be honest, some of the best memories of my time at school have taken place there."

As we have seen in their accounts, the memories of staff and pupils are testament to the quality of the exchanges that visits to the Mawddach Estuary have inspired. The echoes of Christmas Monteverdi in The Coach House are strong, as are the memories of the CCF party on the Headland organised by Wing Commander Dickson to witness Andy

Cadair: conquered

Turner's acrobatics, or the chilled out History Society weekends curated by Tim Lawrence (A-level History, not required), or the Year 7 trips to the Blue Lake to learn how to skim with Lt. Col. Law.

Looking forward to the next 50 years, what might we anticipate in an enlarged Farchynys domain consisting now of The Coach House, The Barn and The Cottage? Certainly more nymph collecting in Coed Y Brenin, more endurance hikes over the Rhinogs and more atmospheric readings in the Gazebo. We can imagine a range of new attractions and activities for the 150+ Fusties in Year 7, and a whole new web of relationships and new challenges met.

This is the story of a place, a singularly beautiful place and the grammar school from Walsall that made it its second home there 50 years ago. Ian Skidmore observed, "the problem with this magic land is not finding it, but leaving it." But for the Marians who have found it, we can be certain of one thing: this place will never leave them. The story continues....

The vision

"It is intended that every boy in the school should have the opportunity of staying at the centre at least once a year"

Bibliography

Anderson, John S (2004) Queen Mary's 1954-2004, Welshpool Printing Group

Berry, David (2013) The Mawddach Ardudwy Trail, Kittiwake

Burnett, Michael (2013) Walks in and around Barmouth Town, Kittiwake

Christiansen, Rex & Miller R.W. (1971) The Cambrian Railways Volume 1, David and Charles

Davis, Brian E (2012) A Walk Through Time, Amberley Publishing

Ellis, T P (1928) Dolgelley and Llanelltyd, The Welsh Outlook Press

Fletcher, HLV (1955) The Queen's Wales: North Wales, Hodder

Frater, Alexander (1983) Stopping-Train Britain, Hodder and Stoughton

Gillham, John (2010) The Mountains of Snowdonia, 4 The Southern Peaks, Frances Lincoln

Jones, E. Rosalie (1909) A History of Barmouth and its Vicinity, John Evans & Nephew

Lofthouse, Jessica (1970) North Wales for the Country Goer, Robert Hale

Mortlock, Colin (1978) Adventure Education, Ferguson of Keswick

Morris, Jan (1998) Wales, Viking

Napier, Jean and Richards, Alun John (2005) A Tale of Two Rivers, Gwasg Carreg Gwalch

Owen, Hugh J (1950) The Treasures of the Mawddach, Swyddla'r Seren

O'Hanlon, Graham and Jacky (2009) The Mawddach Way

O'Hanlon, Graham and Jacky (2009) Explore The Mawddach Trail

Page, Hugh E (1936) Rambles around the Cambrian Coast, Great Western Railway

Redfern, Roger (2004) Mawddach The Story of Barmouth and its District, The Cottage Press

Redfern, Roger A (1968) Rambles in North Wales, Robert Hale

Rees, Vyvyan (1971) Mid-Western Wales: A Shell Guide, Faber and Faber

Rohrs, H and Tunstall-Behrens, H (1970) Kurt Hahn, Routledge & Kegan Paul

Sale, Richard (1988) Best Walks in North Wales, Constable

Skidmore, Ian (1986) Gwynedd, Robert Hale

Thomas, Edward (2013) Beautiful Wales, Read Books

Ward, Lock's (1949) Barmouth and North Wales, Ward Lock &Co

Wide Horizons (2016) The Impact of Adventure Learning, Wide Horizons

Williams, Michael (2012) On the Slow Train Again, Arrow

Williams, Philip Nanney (2016) Nannau, Llwyn Estates

The Marian, The QMGS School Magazine

Farchynys Duty Log Books, Volumes 1, 2, 3 and 4

Minute Book, Queen Mary's Welsh Centre Management Committee, Secretary - PW Evans

Contributors

This book would not have been possible to produce without the generous contributions of the following members of the Marian community:

Members of staff

Brian Bissell, Philip Blackshaw, Gordon Brudenell, Peter Buckley, Philip Davies, John Edlin, David Hart, Alex Hudson, Stuart Holtam, Keith Howard, Steve Law, Mark Lawson, Tim Lawrence, Tim Swain, John Wilcox, Bev Wragg.

Old Marians

Les Barnfield, Steve Bateman, Neil Boynton, Nick Bridgman, Tony Burton, Mike Causer, Ian Cooksey, Adam Draper, David Etherington, Andrew Elliott, Matt Killian, Graham Lightwood, Steve Parsons, David Rowley, Nicholas Sanders, Christopher Slevin, Roxanne Taylor, Andrew Turner, Ian Trow, Peter Welch, Daniel Williams.

Current pupils:

Year 12: Isaac, Ryan, Aaron, Alex, Matthew and Emily
Year 7: Owen, James, Sarujan, Matthew, Nirav and Luke

Thanks are due:

The Editor is grateful for the help and support from the following:
Gillian Columbine – *Alumnorum et dux et lux* – first amongst equals for complete dedication to the task.
Steve Law and Tim Lawrence: sharing insights from hundreds of visits.

Some other people helped with brilliant ideas, fact checking and heavy lifting various – Diolch a galon!

Chris Bradley, Dennis and Margaret Finch, Ruth Fisher, Gail Hall, Sean Hewlett of Yenworthy Lodge, Somerset, Penny Hunt, Peter Morris, Keith Randall, Sharon Thorpe, Robin Wendell Glover

Picture acknowledgements:

The Editor is grateful to many for providing images for the book including former members of staff Brian Bissell, Peter Buckley, David Hart and Tim Lawrence; former pupils: Tony Burton, Andrew Dickson, Matt Killian, Emily Pitt, David Rowley, Andrew Turner and Daniel Williams.
The Wardens, Steve Law and Alex Hudson deserve special mention for making available their high quality collections.
Thanks to Adam Draper for the wonderful illustration of the The Coach House (pg 109). Numerous other pictures appear by kind permission of *The Walsall Observer*.
We apologise for any omissions.

Creative team:

Editing: Ben Brill, illustrations: Dawn Childs, design: Robin Stannard and production: Cynthia Scott-Clark

A Farchynys timeline

541 mya Cambrian period *the rocks of Farchynys and the Harlech Dome deposited*

485 mya Ordovician period *the rocks of Cadair Idris deposited*

400 mya Silurian period *rock layers folded, faulted and impregnated with gold, manganese, zinc and copper*

2 mya – 10000 ya Pleistocene period *glaciers and meltwater erode the whole landscape*

1158 *Foundation of Cymmer Abbey*

1282 *Edward I constructs Harlech Castle*

1404 *Owain Glyndwr captures Harlech Castle and holds a parliament*

1555 *The Red Bandits active in Dinas Mawddwy*

1834 *Gold rush in Bontddu; the boom period is the 1860s - 500 miners working*

1829 *Charles Darwin in Caerdeon; 2 years before setting off on the Beagle*

1824 *William Wordsworth visits the Mawddach*

1795 *Corsy Gedol hotel opens. The first bathing machines arrive in Barmouth*

1794 *Samuel Taylor Coleridge (right) climbs Cadair*

1765 *Richard Wilson's picture of Cader: Lyn-y-Cau inspires Turner*

1757 *Thomas Gray's The Bard inspires a Celtic revival and interest in exploring Wales.*

1856 *Tennyson climbs Cadair*

1867 *Barmouth Bridge opens on 10th October and is rebuilt in 1901*

1869 *Charles Darwin writes The Descent of Man in Caerdeon*

1870-76 *Farchynys Hall and Coach House built by Thomas Oliver*

1957 *Frank Cocksey the Barmouth sculptor and artist buys the Hall*

1876 *John Ruskin visits Barmouth – Fanny Talbot gifts 12 cottages*

1956 *Appointment of S L Darby (above) – the development of QM became his life's work*

1879 *Toll bridge opens at Penmaenpool*

1954 *Queen Mary Grammar School Quatercentenary*

1895 *Dinas Oleu on the Barmouth rock becomes the first property donated to the National Trust*

1952 *The Hall Brothers control the great Mawddach hotels and Inns*

1911 *Mines excavated under The Coach House and the Boat House Cliffs*

1951 *Snowdonia – UK's 3rd National Park opened*

1937 *The Oliver family sold the estate in packets. Mrs Morley buys the Hall*

1941 *Kurt Hahn founds the first Outward Bound Centre at Aberdyfi*

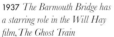

1937 *The Barmouth Bridge has a starring role in the Will Hay film, The Ghost Train*

Marians on the Mawddach   *113*

1962 *SLD hears Kurt Hahn speak at a conference in Oxford*

1963 *Spring: purchase of Farchynys.* **22nd November** *assassination of JFK and launch of The Beatles' second album, With the Beatles.* **23rd November** *the first episode of Doctor Who is broadcast and the first convoy is dispatched with Lt. Col Bull (on the left, in the image on the right) in command.* **29th November** *the first ever party arrives at The Coach House. Jack Aspinall, an Old Marian and Governor and Chairman of Walsall Lithographic purchases Farchynys Hall.*

1965 *QM moves to Mayfield. Beeching liquidates the Dolgellau-Ruabon line. The Coach House's roof is damaged in a storm.*

1966 *Farchynys acquires central heating. Mike Jackson organises the first Farchynys half marathon. 837 Marians had visited The Coach House since the opening in 1963*

1973 *The Centre for Alternative Technology (CAT) was founded on the site of the disused Llwyngwern slate quarry near Machynlleth*

1974 *The Extension is built - Mrs Lindon-Morris, the architect. The Cadair Idris room opens*

1974-76 *Years of drought on the Mawddach. Several weekends cancelled. A secret supply is discovered: "You have more water that Bontddu"*

1983 *The first Grea Farchynys Cycle Ride*

1982 *Farchynys Hall purchased by Alan and Ruth Fisher*

1981 *Other schools paying "an economic rate" to use The Coach House – possibilities of a steady and substantial income?*

1980 *The Coach House connected to mains water supply at last*

1980-86 *Barmouth Bridge closed due to woodworm*

1979 *Farchynys Hall is sold and becomes a boutique hotel and restaurant with implications for usage and behaviour*

1984 *This year 500 boys visit in 41 parties; accompanied by 22 members of staff; Mr Gordon produces the first sequences of a 'videotape' designed to introduce Farchynys to new parents*

1985 *Severe weather disrupts use: 4 trips cancelled, including the Half Marathon. School choir performs Vivaldi's Gloria at Barmouth Parish Church, further strengthening community links.*

1987 *Boys showers and toilets renovated; students from Walsall College of Art combine adventure with some free decorating. The War of the Rhodies begins in earnest.*

1988 *25th anniversary of Farchynys and Sam Darby plants oak trees on the hillside to mark it.*

1997 *Planting of oak trees on the Headland*

1998 *The retirement of Ken Yates. (He died in 1999)*

2006/7 *A major refurbishment at The Coach House: new roof, kitchen and staff bedrooms; dormitory insulated. A very 'challenging' bunk assembly weekend held to commission new, safer bunks*

2017 *The Farchynys estate grows with the acquisition of The Cottage and The Barn*

2016 *First 'Girls Only' weekend*

2015 *Farchynys expansion campaign launched*

2013 *A new smaller dorm added within the Cadair Room - The Cregennan Room*

2011 *CCF conducts first Desert Warfare exercise*

2011 *Dormitory and showers renovated*

A l l t / r   B o e t h

per's Cottage

a-allen

Sheepfold

F.P.

Sheepfold

Farchynys-fach

B.M.
11.1

Farchynys

Floods

Penrhyn Cregyn

R Y